Which are a Shadow of Things to Come; but the Body is of Christ

THE TRUTH
ABOUT
THE SABBATH
OCK SOO PARK

A woman was caught in the act of committing adultery and brought before Jesus. The people who dragged this woman to Jesus asked Him a question: "Master, this woman was taken in adultery, in the very act. Now Moses in the law commanded us, that such should be stoned: but what sayest thou?" Then, Jesus did something in front of them. He wrote on the ground with His finger. There were exactly two times within the Bible when God wrote with His finger. The first time was when God wrote the Ten Commandments that were given to Moses with His finger. He wrote the Ten Commandments on tablets of stone. The second time was when Jesus wrote on the ground with His finger. People are curious about why Jesus wrote on the ground, and about what He wrote. The Bible tells us about this, precisely. The first thing God wrote with His finger were the Ten Commandments: the law. Deuteronomy chapter 28 states that you will be blessed if you keep the law, but you will be cursed if you do not. When God was giving the people of Israel the law, He asked them whether they would keep the law. The people all answered together, "All that the Lord hath spoken, we will do." (Exodus 19:8) However, there has never been a single person among them who has kept all the laws. Everyone has broken the law. As a result, the people of Israel had to be cursed, according to the promise they made with God. God said in Jeremiah 31:31-34 that He would make a new covenant. The first covenant promised that we would be blessed if we kept all the laws, but we would be cursed if we broke even one law. However, because there was no one who could keep all of the laws, all of the people had to be cursed under the law. The new covenant promises that it is God who is at work, and not man doing something. "I will forgive their iniquity, and I will remember their sin no more." God promised that this new covenant would be given when the time comes. The woman caught in the act of committing adultery broke the law and was sentenced to death. However, right then, God opened the era of the new covenant that He promised. "I will forgive their iniquity, and I will remember their sin no more." God kept the Ten Commandments from being seen. He put the tablets of stone with the Ten Commandments inside of the ark of the covenant. Then He closed the lid and had two angels spread their wings and cover the lid so that the ark of the covenant would not be opened. However, the people of Bethshemesh opened the lid of the ark of the covenant and looked inside of it. As a result, fifty thousand, seventy people were put to death. God closed the law and opened the era of the new covenant. Even though the woman caught in adultery had committed sins, her sins were forgiven according to the words, "I will forgive their iniquity, and I

---

will remember their sin no more." We, too, gain the forgiveness of sins and are justified through the new covenant, not through keeping the law. We unload all burdens of sin and have true rest inside of Jesus, who is the Lord of the Sabbath. "There is therefore now no condemnation to them which are in Christ Jesus, who walk not after the flesh, but after the Spirit. For the law of the Spirit of life in Christ Jesus, hath made me free from the law of sin and death." (Romans 8:1-2)

September, 2021
Good News Gangnam Church

Rev. **Ock Soo Park**

Contents

Chapter 1

The Reason We Must Rest on the Sabbath

The Reason We Must Rest on the Sabbath

I personally own about ten Bibles. I have one in my office, one at my church, one in my room, and one in my bag. The fact that the Bible was mass-produced after Johannes Gutenberg invented the moveable type printing press makes me happy whenever I think about it. Before that, it was very difficult for an individual to own his or her own Bible.

Johannes Gutenberg's mother was a very diligent believer of God, and I heard that it was her lifetime wish to own her own Bible. Johannes Gutenberg invented the moveable type printing press so that he could publish the Bible for his mother. Thanks to that, we are able to purchase the Bible at a low price and hold it in our hands. I tasted a new world that could never be found anywhere else in the world except for within the Bible—the world inside of the Bible completely changed my life. Being able to talk about the Bible is quite beautiful and joyous in itself.

Let's read from the scriptures as we continue. Luke chapter 6, verses 1 through 11 says:

And it came to pass on the second sabbath after the first, that he went through the corn fields; and his disciples plucked the ears of corn, and did eat, rubbing them in their hands. And certain of the Pharisees said unto them, Why do ye that which is not lawful to do on the sabbath days? And Jesus answering them said, Have ye not read so much as this, what David did, when himself was an hungred, and they which were with him; How he went into the house of God, and did take and eat the shewbread, and gave also to them that were with him; which it is not lawful to eat but for the priests alone? And he said unto them, That the Son of man is Lord also of the sabbath. And it came to pass also on another sabbath, that he entered into the synagogue and taught: and there was a man whose right hand was withered. And the scribes and Pharisees watched him, whether he would heal on the sabbath day; that they might find an accusation against him. But he knew their thoughts, and said to the man which had the withered hand, Rise up, and stand forth in the midst. And he arose and stood forth.

Then said Jesus unto them, I will ask you one thing; Is it lawful on the sabbath days to do good, or to do evil? to save life, or to destroy it? And looking round about upon them all, he said unto the man, Stretch forth thy hand. And he did so: and his hand was restored whole as the other. And they were filled with madness; and communed one with another what they might do to Jesus.

A Spiritual Life of Labor, Trying to Become Good

I was born in 1944. The very next year, Korea was liberated from Japan. Then in 1950, when I was six years old, there was a big civil war between North Korea and South Korea. At that time, people lived very pitifully in Korea. In fact, 30% of the kids in my class were orphans. And since there were no men around, many families were unable to farm properly. As a result, there was widespread hunger.

I'm reminded of my childhood whenever I read the story in Luke 6 about how Jesus' disciples broke off grains of wheat, rubbed the wheat together in their hands, and ate it. Before I was saved, when it was time for the wheat to ripen, my friends and I would break off the stalks with our hands. Then we'd find a place in the mountains, roast them in a fire, rub them in our hands, and eat them.

In the Bible, it says that if a hungry person went into someone else's field and used a sickle to harvest the wheat, that would be stealing. However, if he plucks some off with his hands, rubs them together, and then eats them, the Bible says that is not stealing. However, in Korea, both methods are considered stealing.

Before I received salvation, I would steal, and then I would go to church early every morning to beg for that sin to be forgiven. At that point and time in my life, I learned many different things. I learned the Lord's Prayer, the Apostles' Creed, the Ten Commandments, and much more. I also learned how to behave at church. However, I did not know true faith.

Despite attending church diligently, and being aware that it was a sin to rip off and eat wheat from other people's farms, and steal apples and persimmons, I stole a lot of these things with my friends because everything was so tasty. These things remained in my heart as sin and tormented me terribly. I read the Bible, but I could not understand the true meaning of the words. It wasn't just me, either—most pastors did not know the true meaning of the Bible, either, and yet, they taught us.

People who try to keep the Sabbath try not to do any work on the Sabbath. That's because it is what the Bible says to do.

Remember the sabbath day, to keep it holy. Six days shalt thou labour, and do all thy work: But the seventh day is the sabbath of the Lord thy God: in it thou shalt not do any work, thou, nor thy son, nor thy daughter, thy manservant, nor thy maidservant, nor thy cattle, nor thy stranger that is within thy gates: (Exodus 20:8-10).

The commandment that tells people to keep the Sabbath Day is the fourth of the Ten Commandments. I did not know the true meaning of the Ten Commandments, so, I only thought that I had to keep them. And I tried very hard to do so.

When I was 18 years old, God blocked all the paths in my life that were presented to me. I was unable to continue with schooling because I was so poor. Poverty and hunger were difficult; however, the greatest pain was living, day by day, without any hope that things would get any better.

So, in 1962, when I was 18 years old, I applied for the vocational military. The thought of becoming a vocational non-commissioned officer made me so hopeful. I would be able to attend night school as a non-commissioned officer. And with my monthly pay, I would be able to afford the tuition and down the road, graduate college. I would probably be honorably discharged from the military, and then I'd be able to get a job. I thought that I could live out the rest of my life like that. However, the first thing I needed to do was a physical examination. Internal medicine, external medicine, eyes, nose, and mouth: I passed every physical. My physique was not that great, but I did not have any significant defects.

However, I had a problem with the dental exam. At the time, there was a small chip on my front tooth. It wasn't noticeable, and you couldn't even see it unless you looked very closely. I had no idea that the medic would make that into a problem. In the end, the dental officer placed a mark on my exam that was different from the signature he scribbled on my friend's checklist, who was standing right next to me.

I told my friend, "Hey, open your mouth." My friend had fine teeth, but I was disqualified.

So, I approached the dental officer and asked him, "Please help me."

"I cannot help you," he replied. "If it was your molar, I'd let you pass. However, it's right there, on your front tooth. How can I help you with that?" He told me that if I got my tooth fixed, he'd pass me. However, I did not have the money to have it done. The hope I had placed in becoming a vocational non-commissioned officer simply disappeared.

Before that, I thought about working for my uncle, who was running a business in Japan. However, Korea and Japan did not have any diplomatic ties at the time, so going there was not feasible. I even considered boarding a smuggler's vessel to get to Japan, but that would not be very easy to do. I fell deep into despair. I thought God was cursing me because I had committed so many sins, but I did not know how to receive the forgiveness of sins. Therefore, even though I attended church, I continued to remain in sin. And even though I attended church, I didn't know how to believe. I just simply tried not to commit sins and be good. I thought living this way was what spiritual life actually was.

The Korean Bible is 1,800 pages long. It has no pictures, and it is only packed with words. I read and understood what was written in the Bible, but I did not know what the words truly meant. What I learned in church was that you had to constantly repent of the sins you committed, be good, serve diligently, pray hard, and give offerings.

This is how many people who go to church today live their spiritual life. They don't know the meaning of the thick Bible as a whole—they only know bits and pieces of it, and do not have a deep understanding of what God is actually saying. They commit sins and pray for those sins to be washed and forgiven. However, even though they do so, they are not sure and are unclear whether their sins are completely washed away or not. I also had lived my spiritual life that way.

The Bible, Which Becomes Understood When Verses and Their Mates Are Found

I was living in despair, but I then experienced a moment in time when I read the Bible with a set of eyes other than my own. For the most part, people who go to church think that if you keep the Ten Commandments well, you will be blessed. I, too, tried to keep the Ten Commandments: "You shall have no other gods before me. You shall not make idols unto yourselves. You shall not take the Lord God's name in vain. You shall remember the Sabbath to keep it holy. Honor thy parents. Thou shalt not murder. Thou shalt not commit adultery. Thou shalt not steal. Thou shalt not give false testimony. Thou shalt not covet."

However, I told many lies. My friends and I would steal apples from other people's farms. I stole many times myself. In this state of a sinner, I tried hard to keep the

Ten Commandments, but always failed. That's when I started reading the Bible.

I could read the entire Bible, cover to cover, in 60 hours. So, I could finish the Bible if I did nothing for an entire week. Then, I ended up reading the Bible, again and again. Isaiah chapter 34, verse 16 goes like this,

Seek ye out of the book of the LORD, and read: no one of these shall fail, none shall want her mate: for my mouth it hath commanded, and his spirit it hath gathered them.

Because the Bible is the Word of God, it says that there is nothing that the Bible lacks, nor is there any verse without its mate.

What is a mate? A woman cannot have a baby by herself. Yes, the woman is the one who gives birth, but she must have a man in order to conceive. It is when a man and woman come together that a new and complete life begins.

My wife and I got married. The best thing that my wife did after getting married was give birth to a beautiful daughter and a handsome son. That is something I could never, ever do myself. It was only possible through our marriage. Just as a man and woman become mates in order to become a married couple and have children, when you read verses in the Bible and cannot understand them, you will be able to realize their meanings when you find their scriptural mates. When you do not know a verse's mate within the Bible, you will only know one side. In that case, no matter how much you may know, you do not fully know the verse.

There were many things I didn't understand in the Bible, no matter how much I read. However, when I found the verses' mates, those scriptures came together. Only then was I able to properly understand the Bible. No matter how great a man is, or how beautiful a woman may be, they cannot have a child by themselves. A man and woman become mates, and that is when they become complete. When God wrote the Bible, the Bible tells us that He wrote it so that every verse of the Scriptures has its mate.

Today, we read about the Sabbath Day in Luke chapter 6. We can also read about the Sabbath Day in the Old Testament, too. What are the mating scriptures regarding the Sabbath Day? What is the true meaning of the Sabbath? Why should one not work on the Sabbath Day? When I was asked these questions, before, all I could answer was, "Well, God said you should not work on that day, so you shouldn't work." However, I wanted to find the mating verses regarding the Sabbath Day. If I know the mating scriptures regarding the Sabbath Day, I will know the true meaning of the Sabbath Day.

Why Do They Lay Their Hands on the Head of the Lamb?

After discovering the mating scriptures I was looking for in the Bible, the words led my heart in amazing ways. This is not only true with the Sabbath Day—it is also true with the law and the forgiveness of sins. When you look at the rules about the sin offering in the Old Testament, when a person committed a sin, he or she had to bring a goat or a lamb to the tabernacle in order to receive the forgiveness of sins. The person would then have to lay his or her hand upon the head of the offering. I did not understand that heart. I asked myself, "Why did they lay their hands on its head? The laying on of hands is done to ordain pastors and elders, but why are they doing it to the lamb? I don't think they're ordaining the lamb to be a pastor or elder."

A long time ago, I wanted clarity on how our sins became forgiven. So, I began to search throughout the Bible for the words that were written about the forgiveness of sins. First of all, Leviticus chapter 4 talks about the sin offering. There are four kinds of sin offerings: the offering given when a priest committed sin, when the entire congregation of Israel sinned, when the ruler of a tribe sinned, and when a common person has sinned. The methods and requirements of these four offerings were all different. This was all recorded in Leviticus chapter 4. At that moment, I was a common person, so, I read the Bible closely to learn how a common person received the forgiveness of sins.

Leviticus chapter 4, verses 27 to 29 talk about the sin offering for the common person:

And if any one of the common people sin through ignorance, while he doeth somewhat against any of the commandments of the Lord concerning things which ought not to be done, and be guilty; Or if his sin, which he hath sinned, come to his knowledge: then he shall bring his offering, a kid of the goats, a female without

*blemish, for his sin which he hath sinned. And he shall
lay his hand upon the head of the sin offering, and slay
the sin offering in the place of the burnt offering.*

Here, it talks about doing the laying on of hands upon
the head of the goat. I asked myself, "Why do they do the
laying on of hands upon the head of the goat?" I needed
to find the mating scriptures for these verses. I had no
idea why they did the laying on of hands. After this, I
read the Old and New Testaments several more times, but
I couldn't find the answer. Even though I had already read
it, I didn't know it was the mate scripture, and just passed
over it. But later on, I discovered something amazing
while I continued to read. Leviticus 16:21 recorded
precisely the reason for this:

*And Aaron shall lay both his hands upon the head of
the live goat, and confess over him all the iniquities of
the children of Israel, and all their transgressions in all
their sins, putting them upon the head of the goat, and
shall send him away by the hand of a fit man into the
wilderness:*

In the Old Testament, if a person committed a sin, a
lamb or a goat was put to death in the place of that person.
However, the lamb or the goat could not just be killed.
The committed sin had to first be placed on the offerings.
This had to be done so the offerings could die for the sins
that were committed. It was the laying on of hands that
transferred the sin onto the offerings. Leviticus chapter
16, verse 21 explains that the sins that were committed
were laid onto the goat by way of the laying on of hands.
This means that through the laying on of hands upon the

offering's head, the person's sin was transferred to the head of the goat.

On the other hand, it doesn't matter how many times you kill a lamb. If the person's sin has not been placed onto the lamb without the laying on of the sinner's hands, the death of the lamb would be meaningless. After telling the lamb, "Lamb, I'm sorry, but can you die instead of me? Please receive my sin," and placing the sins on it by putting your hands on its head, you then had to take a knife and kill the lamb. The lamb has died to officially pay the price for any committed sin.

This is also mentioned in the New Testament. In Matthew chapter 3, John the Baptist is baptizing people in the Jordan River. He shouted to the people, "Repent, the kingdom of heaven is near!" People would go to him, repent of their sins, and be baptized by John the Baptist. However, one day, Jesus came to Jordan River, and said, "John, baptize me." John was shocked. He was Jesus, the holy Son of God.

"I have need to be baptized of thee, and comest thou to me?" John replied.

Jesus answered, "Suffer it to be so now, for thus it becometh us to fulfill all righteousness."

Jesus told John the Baptist that he needed to baptize Him in order to fulfill all righteousness. How does receiving a baptism fulfill all righteousness? And, since Jesus was without sin, there was no need for Him to die due to sin. However, Jesus wanted to die for our sins and make us righteous. But in order for Jesus to die for our sins, our sins needed to be placed on Him, like they did in the Old Testament. Without that happening, Jesus' death would have nothing to do with us.

John the Baptist gave people the baptism of repentance. However, since Jesus did not have any sins, He actually did not need to receive the baptism of repentance. If that is the case, then why did He receive the baptism? This was the process, through which, all our sins were placed on Jesus in order to fulfill all righteousness.

John the Baptist was a qualified priest. Because John's father was a priest, he was also a priest. After John laid his hands on the head of Jesus, right then, the Holy Spirit came down like a dove from heaven. This story is recorded in detail in Matthew chapter 3. However, John chapter 1, verse 29 also mentions this: *The next day John seeth Jesus coming unto him, and saith, Behold the Lamb of God, which taketh away the sin of the world.*

When we read this verse alone, we cannot understand it. But we can understand it all very well when we come to know, through reading the Bible, how sin is transferred to the sin offering through the laying on of hands; how Jesus was without sins and did not need to repent, yet He was baptized by John the Baptist. And when we come to know how that baptism was not a baptism of repentance, but one to fulfill all righteousness by placing every sin of the world onto Jesus when John the Baptist laid his hands on His head. John saw Jesus coming to him and said, "Behold, the Lamb of God which takes away the sin of the world." As the verses of the Bible, and all their mates, came together, one by one, I came to precisely understand the Bible.

The Shadow of Things to Come; the Body Is Jesus Christ.

Now let us talk about the Sabbath Day again. The book of Exodus talks about the Sabbath:

Remember the sabbath day, to keep it holy. Six days shalt thou labour, and do all thy work: But the seventh day is the sabbath of the Lord thy God: in it thou shalt not do any work, thou, nor thy son, nor thy daughter, thy manservant, nor thy maidservant, nor thy cattle, nor thy stranger that is within thy gates: (Exodus 20:8-10)

This is the rules of the Sabbath Day that were written in the Old Testament. Many churches today are working hard trying to keep the Sabbath Day. I began to search throughout the Bible because I wanted to learn more about the Sabbath Day. I discovered something very important in Colossians chapter 2, verse 16: *Let no man therefore judge you in meat, or in drink, or in respect of an holyday, or of the new moon, or of the sabbath days.* And the next verse, verse 17 reads, *Which are a shadow of things to come; but the body is of Christ.* Keeping the Sabbath Day, itself, is not the real thing. It is a shadow that reveals something else that will come in the future. You could never know this if you only read the rules of the Sabbath Day in Exodus, and not the book of Colossians.

In the Bible, a new day would begin at sunset. When the sun sets on Friday, the Sabbath Day begins. Then it is the Sabbath Day until the sun sets on Saturday. Is this the real thing or a shadow? It's a shadow. If that is the case, then it is laughable to try to keep the Sabbath Day.

It is only a shadow of something else. Isn't that what Colossians is clearly telling us? It says that the Sabbath Day is a shadow.

"Is keeping the Sabbath Day the right thing to do?" People may think this way when they look at only one part of the Bible. But we have to find the scriptures and their mates to know the precise meaning. When a person who has a proper understanding of the Bible speaks, and the listeners do not know the word precisely, they will call the speaker a heretic and all kinds of nonsense. That is because they don't understand the fact that they don't know the Bible precisely. It is not that we should only know, "You shall remember the Sabbath Day to keep it holy." We have to know the other aspects of the Sabbath precisely as well.

Colossians is a mate scripture: *Let no man therefore judge you in meat, or in drink, or in respect of an holyday, or of the new moon, or of the sabbath days. (Colossians 2:16)* This is telling us not to argue and fight over the new moons, holidays, or the sabbath days. Why is that? It is because those things are not the real things, but a shadow of things to come. *Which are a shadow of things to come; but the body is of Christ. (Colossians 2:17)*

If there is a shadow, there is a body, in other words, the real thing. To what is the Sabbath Day a shadow? The body is Jesus Christ. God has spoken through the law what would happen in the future when Jesus comes. In Exodus, they killed the Passover lamb. When they put the blood of the lamb on the side doorposts and the upper post, the firstborn of that home would get to live.

However, the firstborn would die in the houses where the blood was not put on the doorpost. The blood represents Jesus Christ. It is teaching us how He shed His blood and died for us. And that is what saves us from destruction.

I Will Give You Rest

If so, then what is the true meaning of the Sabbath Day? In order to reveal what we are unable to see right now and to show us the things that are to come, God made the Sabbath Day. The same way that you can look at the shadow and know the shape of the actual body, God used the Sabbath Day, which is a shadow, to teach us something: Jesus Christ. We live struggling with the heavy load of sin.

There is a hymn that goes like this: "I cannot bear these burdens alone. In my distress, he kindly will help me." Like the lyrics state, you were carrying very heavy loads and burdens, but once you arrive at the Sabbath Day, you get to let go of them all. It means that once Jesus comes and you meet Him, you will be freed from all the burden of your sin.

No matter how well you keep the Sabbath Day, that is not doing the will of God. Did Jesus keep the Sabbath Day? No, He did not. He worked on the Sabbath. He healed the sick. The disciples broke off wheat and ate them. Breaking off the wheat is harvesting and rubbing them together in their hands is threshing. The Pharisees saw this and said, "Why do you do that which is not lawful on the Sabbath Day?" which is saying, "You violated the Sabbath." To the Pharisees who asked this, Jesus answered, "The son of man is the Lord of the Sabbath."

When the sun sets on the evening of every Friday, the Sabbath Day begins and all the heavy loads are dropped. This is a shadow of the greater thing to come, and the actual "thing" is Jesus. You are able to let go of all your heavy loads and become free as soon as the Sabbath Day begins. This means that once you meet Jesus, you get to unload your load of sin and be free. This is what the Sabbath Day teaches.

A long time ago, I went to Israel. One day, I went to the Wailing Wall. It was the Sabbath Day. A member of our church was diligently taking pictures of the temple wall, but the security guard came to him and told him to stop. When he asked why he was not allowed to take photos, the guard said, "You cannot press down on the shutter button because it's the Sabbath." He was saying you should not work. Our church member's friend heard everything and asked the security guard, "Then why do you press on the walkie-talkie? That looks like work, too. Don't just tell us to keep the Sabbath."

People do this because they do not fully know the true meaning of the Sabbath Day; they don't know the true meaning of the words of the Bible. They could memorize all 66 books of the Bible, but that is not knowing the Bible. Through the Sabbath Day, God is revealing how Jesus was going to come to this world in the future. It is showing us that Jesus would come and free us from all our sins. Once Jesus comes, we get to shed the load of our sin.

A long time ago, the servants in Israel would carry heavy loads and struggle with them all day long. Then when the sun was about to set on Friday evening, they would say, "The sun is setting. The sun has set!" This is when the servant could let go of all of his heavy loads. Likewise, when we come before Jesus, we get to let go of all the heavy loads of our sins. Today, many people in churches say, "Lord, I'm a sinner. Please forgive me." Carrying their load of sin and being in pain is violating the Sabbath. Why? The true meaning of the Sabbath Day is to be freed from the load of sin.

Jesus said, *Come unto me all you who labor and are heavy laden, and I will give you rest.* When we come before Jesus, all of our sins are washed away, and we are freed from sin. Some people boast that they're able to keep the Sabbath Day well. Those people don't know how to keep the Sabbath Day. They have no faith. These people are holding onto the shadow. In the Old Testament, it says to keep the Sabbath Day. However, the mate scripture to that verse is in Colossians. There, the Sabbath Day is taught to be the shadow of things to come.

We must find mate scriptures in the Bible such as this one in order to learn their true meanings.

How Can You Be Freed from Your Heavy Load of Sin?

On the Sabbath Day, everyone lets go of their heavy loads. Then how can we come before Jesus to let go of the load of sin and be freed from sin? When we believe in Jesus, we can be freed from sin and have true freedom. On October 7, 1962, I amazingly received the forgiveness of sins by the blood of Jesus. From then on, the eyes I saw the scriptures with were completely different from my own.

The woman caught in the act of committing adultery appears in John chapter 8. The scribes and Pharisees dragged this woman to Jesus and said, "This woman was caught in the act of adultery. Moses in the law commanded that such a woman should be stoned. But sir, what sayest thou?" There is no mercy in the law. There is only curse and destruction. When this woman who committed adultery was judged by the law, she could only be stoned to death.

However, this woman was not judged by the law, but came before Jesus. What did Jesus say to this woman? "Woman, where are those thine accusers? Hath no man condemned thee?" When the woman lifted up her head and looked around, the people who wanted to stone her were no longer there. There were just stones the size of fists littering the ground. She realized, "Ah, those stones were supposed to have been flying towards me. They should have broken my head and broken my nose. And I should be bled out and dead." Jesus again spoke to this woman, "Neither do I condemn thee. Go and sin no more." Jesus saved this woman from the stones that were meant to fly at her.

"Come unto me all ye who labor and are heavy laden, and I will give you rest." These are such amazing words. This woman had no choice but to be stoned and killed, but Jesus put her sins upon Himself. That was how He saved this woman from her sins. When Jesus received the laying on of hands from John, all of our sins were placed on Jesus. John the Baptist saw Jesus and said, "Behold, the Lamb of God who takes away the sin of the world." When the person who committed sin laid his hands upon the head of the goat, the sin would then be placed on the head of the goat. Which one dies after this is done? Does the one who committed the sin die, or does the goat die? The person who committed the sin is not killed—the goat is the one who dies.

Did the woman taken in the act of adultery die for the judgement of her sins? No, she did not die. The sin was committed by the woman taken in the act of adultery, but it was Jesus who was crucified. That is because Jesus carried the sins of the woman taken in the act of adultery. This woman was freed from sin. Jesus not only put upon Himself the sins of this woman taken in the act of adultery, but also the sins of Pastor Ock Soo Park. Jesus carried all of our sins and died on the cross. It is not that we need to do something. We simply need to look to the cross and believe in Jesus. "Ah, Jesus shed His blood and died on the cross in order to receive the punishment for my sins instead of me. That is where my sins ended. I'm clean. I'm holy." Believing this means believing in Jesus.

Isn't It Arrogant to Say That You Have No Sins?

I received the forgiveness of sins in 1962. My eldest sister was seven years older than I was. We didn't have our mother, so my oldest sister basically raised me. Because we attended church together, I spoke with her after receiving the forgiveness of sins. I said, "Sister, all of my sins have been washed clean."

She then became wide-eyed, and replied, "Ock Soo, you're in big trouble. The more spiritual life you have the humbler you must become. Even the pastor says he's a sinner, and the elder says he's a sinner, too. Does it make any sense for you to say that you have no sins? Ripe fruit bows down lower. If you have faith, you should be humble. How could you be so arrogant and say that you have no sins?" I didn't have a reply for her.

I visited the place where my then-church's choir members gathered, and I told them that I received the forgiveness of sins. The choir members who listened to me said, "Mr. Park, I'm like that, too. I have sin, so what am I supposed to do?" I can answer this question well now, but I was unable to back then. People then began to ostracize me because I continually brought it up in church.

Back then, there was a room at the church where the youth hung out. Once, I was about to walk through the door of that room, and there were all these shoes laid out. I heard a friend of mine talking about me inside the room. "Ock Soo Park is such a joke," he said. "I know him. And he says that he has no sins?" He was a friend that I used to steal and often do bad things with. It was true that he knew me very well. However, all the sins that I had committed were forgiven by the blood of Jesus. My friend called me a joke because he did not know this fact.

Since every person at that church was a sinner, I ended up ostracized. At that time, God paved the way for me to go to a missionary school run by born-again missionaries.

If You Are a Sinner, It Means That Jesus Failed

If you're still a sinner, that means Jesus died in vain. Jesus died to wash away our sins, so if your sins still remain, it means He failed. Some people say that they saw a vision when explaining how they received the forgiveness of sins. Some people say they had tears streaming down their faces and runny noses. However, our sins were washed away at the cross where Jesus was crucified.

In Isaiah chapter 53, verse 6, it says, *All we like sheep have gone astray; we have turned every one to his own way; and the LORD hath laid on him the iniquity of us all.* In this verse, "him," is Jesus. God hath laid all of our sins on Jesus. Jesus carried all of our sins and paid the price for all of them.

Isaiah chapter 53, verses 4 and 5 read,

Surely he hath borne our griefs, and carried our sorrows: yet we did esteem him stricken, smitten of God, and afflicted. But he was wounded for our transgressions, he was bruised for our iniquities: the chastisement of our peace was upon him; and with his stripes we are healed.

All of our sins were resolved at the cross. Believing in this is believing in Jesus. Isaiah chapter 44, verse 22 explains this in a more visual way. *I have blotted out, as a thick cloud, thy transgressions, and, as a cloud, thy sins: return unto me; for I have redeemed thee.*

According to this verse, which comes first, us returning to God, or God blotting out our sins? The blotting out is first. To blot something out means to erase it by painting over it. If you look at the rules of the sin offering in Leviticus chapter 4, the lamb has to bleed out and die after laying one's hands on the lamb and placing the sin on it (making the lamb a sin offering). Then, the blood of the lamb is applied to the horns of the altar. My initial question was, "Why did they put the blood upon the horns of the altar?" I discovered the reason while reading the Bible. After reading it ten, 20, and 30 times, I came to know the structure of the Bible as a whole. Then, as I read the Bible 40, 50, and 60 times, the words in it fit with each other, one by one. It was so amazing.

I searched carefully to see why the blood of the lamb was applied to the horns of the altars. The mate scripture was in Jeremiah chapter 17. *The sin of Judah is written with a pen of iron, and with the point of a diamond: it is graven upon the table of their heart, and upon the horns of your altars. (Jeremiah 17:1)* God recorded our sins in two places: one on God's end and the other on man's end. For example, suppose I made watches and sold them. Suppose Pastor Joseph Park, who is my language interpreter, purchases my watches and sells them. However, one day, Pastor Joseph Park was short on money, so he bought $50,000 worth of watches from me on credit. Then, he needs to write everything down in his ledger, and I also need to write it down in my ledger. We will both look at our own documents, and Pastor Joseph

Park would think, "I need to pay this bill." And I would think to myself, "Why hasn't he paid for this yet?" But, when he pays me the $50,000, I cross out the record from my ledger, and he crosses out the record on his ledger. This is how our sins are resolved as well.

Our sins are recorded on the table of our hearts and on the horns of the altars. On our end, sin is recorded on the tables of our hearts. That is why we remember the sins we have committed in our hearts. On God's end, they are recorded on the horns of the altars. That's why you put the blood the lamb upon the horns of the altar after it is killed and given as an offering.

This is talked about in Leviticus chapter 4. We'll look at Leviticus chapter 4, verses 27 and 28:

And if any one of the common people sin through ignorance, while he doeth somewhat against any of the commandments of the LORD concerning things which ought not to be done, and be guilty; or if his sin, which he hath sinned, come to his knowledge; then he shall bring his offering, a kid of the goats, a female without blemish, for his sin which he hath sinned. Because the wages of sin is death, the person who committed sin has to bring the goat that would be put do death. *And he shall lay his hand upon the head of the sin offering, and slay the sin offering in the place of the burnt offering. (Leviticus 4:29)*

Earlier, we spoke about how the laying on of hands signified the transfer of sin onto the goat. After the sin has been placed onto the goat, the goat is put to death. The blood of that goat is placed on the horns of the altar. *And the priest shall take of the blood thereof with his finger, and put it upon the horns of the altar of burnt offering, and shall pour out all the blood thereof at the bottom of the altar. (Leviticus 4:30)*

The reason the blood is put on the horns of the altar is because the goat's death has paid the price of the sin. The records of sin are erased by the blood that covers them. This is what it means to blot them out. The blood of Jesus Christ erases all the records of sin in heaven. If so, what erases the sin recorded on the tables of the heart? "I stole. I lied. I did evil." These things are erased through faith. Jesus was crucified, died, and washed away all of my sins. When you believe that, they are all washed away. A person who still thinks that he is a sinner because there is no faith that the blood of Jesus has washed his or her sins away.

Our sins have all been washed away through the blood that Jesus shed on the cross. However, when people don't know this, they say they are sinners. Because I cannot check for myself whether I have sins or not, I look at the Bible, which is the Word of God. The Bible says the record of our sins have all been erased. It says that nowhere in heaven is there any record of sins that remain. Another important thing to consider is that God does not remember our sins.

Let us read Jeremiah chapter 31, verse 34 together: *... saith the LORD: for I will forgive their iniquity, and I will remember their sin no more.* Does God remember our sins? He does not. This is because the judgement for our sins has ended. There is nothing more insulting to Jesus than you stating that you're a sinner. That is not being humble. It is insulting Jesus. It is simply saying Jesus failed to wash away all of our sins at the cross.

The Punishment for All Sins Ended at the Cross

God has portrayed Jesus from the book of Genesis. God wrote about how Jesus would die on the cross to wash away all of our sins. According to those words, Jesus came to this earth 2,000 years ago. He was baptized by John the Baptist so that all the sins of mankind could be placed upon Him. Jesus received the punishment for sins by being crucified and shedding His blood.

When a prosecutor asks for sentencing in court, they do not like the use the word, "death penalty." Instead, they express themselves by saying, "In order to protect society, the state asks for the highest punishment permissible by the law." The highest punishment permissible under law is the death penalty.

Now I would like to ask you, suppose a person killed someone, and was sentenced to the death penalty and was executed. But later on, if it was revealed that he had killed an additional person—what would happen then? Do they revive that executed person and kill him again? Because the death penalty is the highest punishment, then whether you killed a single person or two people or 100 people, you will get the death penalty.

The sins of all mankind were placed upon Jesus, and Jesus was executed. Therefore, no more punishment remains. The punishment for sins ended through the crucifixion of Jesus. Therefore, God sees us and says that we're sanctified. The horns of the altars have been covered with the blood, meaning the records of our sins have been erased. And the sins recorded in our hearts are erased through faith. It is true that I have lied, and it is true that I have done evil things, but Jesus received the punishment for all these sins. The judgment for my sins already ended on the cross. That's why God says that I'm righteous in the Bible. This is what it means to believe.

In Romans chapter 3, verse 23 and 24, it says, *For all have sinned, and come short of the glory of God; Being justified freely by his grace through the redemption that is in Christ Jesus.* The grace of Jesus, freely given, allows God to look at Pastor Ock Soo Park and say, "You are justified." The young lady sitting in audience here is also justified. The young man sitting over there in the audience is also justified. This lady with the glasses is also justified. God says you're justified. That means you're righteous.

On the other hand, if you say that you are a sinner, you are insulting the cross. I believe the blood of Jesus washed away all of my sins. God said in the Bible, *I have blotted out, as a thick cloud, thy transgressions, and, as a cloud, thy sins: return unto me; for I have redeemed thee. (Isaiah 44:22)* Which comes first? The blotting out? Or the returning? The blotting out comes first. God is saying, "Because I have blotted your sins out, and because I have already washed away your sins and made you righteous and holy, return to me."

Pastors of many churches, today, misunderstand the Bible—they say that even though Jesus has forgiven our sins, we are still sinners. Do not be fooled. The Bible says that we are justified. It says that our sins have been washed clean. Everyone, are you still a sinner? We were dirty sinners, but we have been washed as white as snow through the blood of Jesus. It is not that we did anything. Jesus did it.

The Bible says, *Come unto me, all ye that labor and are heavy laden, and I will give you rest. (Matthew 11:28)* Hallelujah. I believe this amazing truth. I'm so excited to talk about this. Everyone, are all of you righteous? Happy day, happy day, when Jesus washed my sins away. I praise the Lord.

Chapter 2

Could We Be Like the Good Samaritan?

Could We Be Like the Good Samaritan?

I cannot say how thankful I am that we can speak with an open Bible in front of us. The whole world is going through difficulties due to COVID-19. I hope that the Word of God will enter your heart, and you will be able to overcome it. That will bring peace and happiness to your hearts. We will read from Luke chapter 10, starting from verse 25:

And, behold, a certain lawyer stood up, and tempted him, saying, Master, what shall I do to inherit eternal life? He said unto him, What is written in the law? how readest thou? And he answering said, Thou shalt love the Lord thy God with all thy heart, and with all thy soul, and with all thy strength, and with all thy mind; and thy neighbour as thyself. And he said unto him, Thou hast answered right: this do, and thou shalt live. But he, willing to justify himself, said unto Jesus, And who is my neighbour? And Jesus answering said, A certain man went down from Jerusalem to Jericho, and fell among thieves, which stripped him of his raiment, and wounded him, and departed, leaving him half dead. And by chance there came down a certain priest that way: and when he saw him, he passed by on the other side. And likewise a Levite, when he was at the place, came and looked on him, and passed by on the other side. But a certain Samaritan, as he journeyed, came where he was: and when he saw him, he had compassion on him, and went to him, and bound up his wounds, pouring in oil and wine, and set him on his own beast, and brought him to an inn, and took care of him. And on the morrow when he departed, he took out two pence, and gave them to the host, and said unto him, Take care of him; and whatsoever thou spendest more, when I come again, I will repay thee. Which now of these three, thinkest thou, was neighbour unto him that fell among the thieves? And he said, He that shewed mercy on him. Then said Jesus unto him, Go, and do thou likewise. (Luke 10:25-37)

The Path of Going Forward Strengthened by Jesus Christ

We talked about the Sabbath Day in chapter 1. Many people read the Bible, but live a spiritual life of labor and trying to keep the Sabbath Day because they don't know exactly why God gave us the Sabbath.

Like I mentioned earlier, in the Bible, there are mate scriptures. If you look at the Bible myopically, you cannot properly understand it. You can attain clear understanding of its meaning when mate scriptures of the Bible come together.

The Korean Bible consists of about 1,800 pages. It has no pictures. It is packed only with words. If you read the Bible ten hours a day, you can finish the entire book in six days. After I began reading the Bible and read it the 30th time through, I was able to see its overall structure. A new world in the Bible that I had not seen before appeared to me through its pages.

When people first read the Bible, they have the thought, "If I work hard to keep the Ten Commandments, then I will be blessed." However, throughout the history of mankind, not one single person has kept the Ten Commandments perfectly in order to live a good spiritual life. That is why we need Christ, who died instead of us.

There are only two paths for us to come before God. The Bible tells us that one of the two ways is to be strengthened solely by Jesus Christ. However, people think, "I kept the Sabbath Day today. I will be fine if I continue to serve like this." Most people try to come before God through their own effort and works.

I have read many books on spiritual life, and I have read books written by famous people. However, those books do not often speak precisely to what the words of the Bible say, including the fact that Jesus washed away our sins. Isaiah chapter 44, verse 22 says, *I have blotted out, as a thick cloud, thy transgressions, and, as a cloud, thy sins: return unto me; for I have redeemed thee.* The forgiveness of sins must be achieved 100% through Jesus. We must not have the thought that we can go to heaven by keeping the law or by doing something.

Was Going from Jerusalem Down to Jericho

The story of the man who fell among thieves that we read today was told by Jesus. There was a certain man going down from Jerusalem to Jericho when he fell among thieves. Jerusalem is a city built on top of a mountain. At the time of David, the city was called Jebus. When David wanted to conquer the city, the people said, "David, you will not be able to conquer this city. Even the blind and lame will be able to defeat you."

When you look at the history of Israel, there are many stories of cities being conquered. It is difficult to build city walls higher than 20 meters. Therefore, when enemies attack and pile dirt higher than 20 meters, they can climb onto the walls and easily shoot arrows into the city. However, Jerusalem was a city on a mountain. The entire city was on top of a hill surrounded by mountains. They were unable to pile dirt outside of its walls. That's why it was almost impossible to conquer Jebus.

Many people had tried but the city remained safe. After David became king, he planned to build the Temple of Jerusalem that God wanted built. However, how was David going to conquer the city on top of a mountain? David thought about it. There are waterways that bring the water into the city. David ordered his soldiers to infiltrate through the waterways and as a result, he was able to conquer Jebus.

There was a certain person who was traveling from Jerusalem, which was the city on the mount, to Jericho. Jericho had a low altitude, very close to sea-level. There were many trees, such as olive trees, in the city of Jericho. This person was going down from Jerusalem to Jericho and fell among thieves. The thieves stripped him and left him half-dead.

What Is Written and How Do You Read It?

How did this story begin? In Luke chapter 10, verse 25 it says, *And, behold, a certain lawyer stood up, and tempted him, saying, Master, what shall I do to inherit eternal life?*

The lawyer thought that he could do something to inherit eternal life. However, Jesus replied to him like this, "What is written in the law and how readest thou?" This question means that the law can be read one way or another. If Jesus asks, "What is written in the law?" then the lawyer could answer, "It says this." However, Jesus said, "What is written in the law and how readest thou?"

People half-heartedly know the Bible and consider their own thoughts right. This creates differences in opinions and interpretations of the Bible. As a result of that, there are many denominations even though they are all reading the same Bible. This occurs because people read the same Bible from different angles.

The Children of Israel Who Promised That They Could Keep All the Laws

We need to know the Bible precisely in order to live spiritual life. We must precisely know the intention behind what God is saying. However, most people do not read the Bible very much. Even many of the pastors I have met do not read the Bible very deeply. In Exodus chapter 19, God told the people of Israel, "If you keep my laws, then you will be a nation of priests. You will be a blessed people." Right then, the people of Israel answered, "We will keep all of them."

Let us look at Exodus chapter 19, verses 5 through 7:

Now therefore, if ye will obey my voice indeed, and keep my covenant, then ye shall be a peculiar treasure unto me above all people: for all the earth is mine: And ye shall be unto me a kingdom of priests, and an holy nation. These are the words which thou shalt speak unto the children of Israel. And Moses came and called for the elders of the people, and laid before their faces all these words which the Lord commanded him.

Verse 8 contains the response from the people of Israel:

And all the people answered together, and said, All that the LORD hath spoken we will do. And Moses returned the words of the people unto the LORD.

I would like to ask you a question. Has there been one person among the countless born into this world who has been able to keep all the words of God? No, not one person. However, people have an illusion that they can live according to the Word of God if they try hard to do so. The Bible says that you will be blessed if you keep all of the laws. But on the other hand, it says that if you break even one of the laws, you will be cursed. The problem was that the answer of the people of Israel was a determination to keep all the laws—this was a thoughtless answer.

Do you know why people do drugs? People do drugs because they think, "If I really wanted to, I can quit drugs whenever I want." However, they are unable to quit. Do you know why people steal? If they thought they would get caught, they would never steal because they would have to go to prison. A person who has been to prison knows how painful it is to be incarcerated. Therefore, a person will definitely not steal if he or she knows there is a chance of being caught. Someone who believes it is possible to steal will think in his or her heart that they will not get caught if they do it a certain way.

Then, why did the woman who was caught in the act of adultery, commit adultery in John chapter 8? Was it because she had a lustful heart? "Wow, that man is so handsome. I wish I could just spend one night with him." She may have had a lustful heart like that. However, most people do not commit adultery because they know they will get stoned to death if they are caught. However, this woman who committed adultery believed in her thoughts that convinced her, "If I do it discreetly, nobody will know."

I have taught the Bible to inmates in prisons for a decade-plus. There is a common denominator shared by people who enter prisons. They all believed in their own thoughts that told them, "I will not get caught if I do it this way." That is why they are able to commit crimes. If a person knows he or she will surely get caught committing adultery and that the punishment is death by stoning, they will definitely refuse it. Who wants to go through that? This woman had the heart to commit adultery, though, thinking, "If I do it this way, then I will never get caught." She believed that thought.

This is also true with people who gamble. No one gambles to lose money. People have the heart to win money through gambling. The thought of winning money takes up more real estate in their heart than the thought of losing. Even though they lost money gambling the last time, they feel as though they will win if they just play one more time. Eventually, they end up taking money from their children's college savings and use it to gamble. And if they have the confidence to win money, there is no problem putting up the money they have, regardless if it's for something like their child's college tuition. They could even use the money saved for their spouse's operation and spend it on gambling. To them, winning it all could mean winning back what they gambled, many times over. That is why it would not be a problem to them.

However, if they lose, then their wives would not be able to get the surgery they need, and they could possibly die. It should be normal to have this kind of consideration. However, the people who are addicted to gambling only think that they will win. Therefore, they lose all their money, and they tearfully suffer in pain. They lose their houses to gambling, but again, they feel that they will win the next time around. They would not gamble if they thought that losing was a possibility. But they think that they will win, and they are deceived by that thought.

That's why they are able to gamble away their children's college savings, and the money for their spouse's surgery. They want to win, so they believe the heart that makes them feel like they're going to win.

The Youths Who Are Renewed by Learning the World of the Heart in the Bible

There are many problems that arise because of a wrong heart. I have written many books concerning mind education. In 2007, the Chinese Youth League of China invited me regarding the problems of the nation's youth. However, I had other conferences scheduled, so I was unable to go at that time.

I was once again invited in 2009. I went to the Chinese Youth League headquarters in Beijing, and there, I lectured to the youths for two days. The Chinese Youth League trusted me to provide guidance to their youths. And afterwards, we were scheduled to hold the IYF World Camp in Beijing in 2010. However, that never happened.

After I lectured in Beijing, a publishing company in China reached out to me. They said, "The content of your lectures for the Chinese Youth League was so good that we want to compile it into a book and publish it. However, the manuscript is currently too short, so we would like you to expand upon what we have so far so that we can make the book." After I added more content to the manuscript, we published the book in Korea before sending the manuscript to China. That book became a bestseller.

I founded International Youth Fellowship (IYF) in 2001, and I work for the youth. The IYF is a youth organization that teaches and guides young people. When I look at college students, they are young, good looking, and beautiful. They live in an environment so nice compared with that of my generation. However, oftentimes, that is not the reality in their hearts.

One time, I met a student whose heart was in so much darkness. He was in tremendous pain, and I listened to his story. He was living with his stepmother. I often find shades of darkness and pain in the hearts of young people. Some say that they hate their stepmothers, or want to kill their stepfathers after living with them. Their hearts are filled with hatred and pain.

Currently, it is said that the divorce rate in Seoul has exceeded 30%, and is at the cusp of 40%. Even now, the divorce rates are increasing across the world. However, there are rarely ever any divorces in our church. The reason for that is that people barely ever get divorced at our church, and those who were divorced often come to our church and reunite.

About ten years ago, a young lady started attending my church. After she attended for one month, she received the forgiveness of sins and became born again. Her life changed so much, and she was very happy. One day, this lady asked to meet with me, and we sat down, face to face. She told me that two years ago, she was divorced.

I asked her, "Why did you get divorced?"

"My personality did not fit with my husband's personality at all."

"Do you get divorced if your personalities don't fit?"

"Pastor, it's because you don't know my husband. You should try living with him."

"Why would I live with your husband? I like living with my wife," I said, laughing.

She asked me, "Why are you laughing?"

"Sister, you made me laugh."

"Pastor, I didn't make you laugh."

"Yes, you did." Then I explained the situation to her. "When you buy a TV and the volume is too loud while you're watching it, do you just toss the TV out?"

"No," she answered.

"You simply adjust the volume with the remote, correct?"

"Yes."

"Now, suppose you installed an air conditioner. If the room gets too cold, do you just shiver and throw out the air conditioner?"

"No. You adjust the temperature."

"The TV and air conditioner both have functions that allow you to make adjustments. People are built with so much more intricacy than those machines. You are more than capable of making adjustments when you experience discomfort in life."

She told me that her husband was not re-married, so I told her to reconcile with him. Afterwards, her husband visited me, and I spoke with him. The couple had a discussion and decided to reunite. Their parents were very happy with this decision, but above all, the children were the happiest. Now, the family is living very happily.

Couples get divorced when they only think about their own positions. However, the children experience great pain because of this and end up living in darkness. Many youths live like this. I am so thankful when I see them being renewed in the Word of God.

People Who Read the Bible Crookedly and Influenced by Satan

There are many people who know the Bible halfheartedly. Very rarely do people precisely know the Bible. The way for our spirit to live is within the Bible. However, there are many people who only know this halfway, and they interpret the Bible according to their own thoughts.

In the Bible, every verse has its mates. God works when they are connected with one another and the Word has settled in your heart. In Luke chapter 10, the lawyer said, "What good must I do to inherit eternal life?" This lawyer tried to do something himself in order to gain eternal life. However, we do not obtain eternal life through doing something. It is received by grace.

This is what Ephesians chapter 2, verses 1 through 3 say:

And you hath he quickened, who were dead in trespasses and sins; Wherein in time past ye walked according to the course of this world, according to the prince of the power of the air, the spirit that now worketh in the children of disobedience: Among whom also we all had our conversation in times past in the lusts of our flesh, fulfilling the desires of the flesh and of the mind;

and were by nature the children of wrath, even as others.

The Bible tells us that we all follow the spirit that works now in the children of disobedience. That spirit continually leads our hearts on a path contrary to what's written in the Bible. In John chapter 13, verse 2, it says, *The devil, having now put into the heart of Judas Iscariot, the son of Simon, the thought to betray Jesus.* Just as Satan put those thoughts into Judas Iscariot's heart, Satan works the same way in the hearts of everyone today. Many people listen to the voice of Satan, and they read the Bible under his influence. Even though it's the same Bible, it is completely different when you look at it with the thoughts Satan has put into you versus the eyes of God.

The lawyer had a wrong set of eyes. What did the lawyer ask Jesus? He asked, "What good must I do to inherit eternal life?" The lawyer thought he needed to do good deeds in order to receive eternal life. But Jesus replied, *What is written in the law? How readest thou? (Luke 10:26)* Even though it's the same law, He is saying that the law could be read this way or that way. Which means you can read the Bible with one set of eyes or another.

We can be influenced by Satan, who is the prince of the power of the air, which means that it is possible we could understand the Bible in a crooked manner. Because many Christians around the world live their spiritual life with the Bible as the standard, on the surface, it looks like they are following the Word of God. But, they do not follow the words of the Bible accordingly, despite thinking that they, themselves, are not acting contrary to what the Bible inscribes. Satan deceives them, over and over again.

Are We the Savior, or the Ones to Be Saved?

The parable of the man who fell among thieves speaks of a certain man traveling from Jerusalem to Jericho who was attacked by thieves on the way. These thieves beat him, stripped him, and then left him half dead. What does the image of this person being left half dead illustrate? He was unable to move and could do absolutely nothing. This is illustrating the state we are in.

At that moment, a priest walked by, saw this man who was hit by robbers, and passed by on the other side. He said to himself, "This person must have been attacked by thieves. Then those thieves must still be nearby. If something goes wrong, this could happen to me, too." He had that thought, so he quickly ran away. A Levite also passed by, saw him, and ran away, without even looking back. In Luke chapter 10, verse 33, it says, *But a certain Samaritan, as he journeyed, came where he was...* Who was this Samaritan? He represents Jesus. He was ready to die, and He went forward to save the man who was attacked by thieves.

Jesus asked the lawyer, "How do you read the law?" When you read the law, you must conclude that you can't keep the law—that is when you can seek the grace of Jesus instead. A person who thinks that he can keep the law tries to do something good on his own. They go to church on Sundays and even tithe. However, in light of all this, if we could save ourselves on our own, then why would we need Jesus to come to this world?

Two kinds of people exist from within the story of the man who fell among thieves. One is the savior. The other, is the one in need of saving. Is Jesus the savior, or the one who needs saving? He is the savior. Then, are we the savior or the one who needs saving? We need saving. However, today, there are pastors from many churches who teach people that they must be like the good Samaritan. They are truly people who do not know the Bible. How could we save other people? We are people who can't even save ourselves.

Because this person in the audience cannot save himself, the savior is in the Bible. The Samaritan is the savior. The man who fell among thieves is the one who had no choice but to die unless someone saved him. He's the one in need of saving.

But a certain Samaritan, as he journeyed, came where he was: and when he saw him, he had compassion on him, and went to him, and bound up his wounds, pouring in oil and wine, and set him on his own beast, and brought him to an inn, and took care of him. And on the morrow when he departed, he took out two pence, and gave them to the host, and said unto him, Take care of him; and whatsoever thou spendest more, when I come again, I will repay thee. (Luke 10:33-35)

Let's talk a little bit more on this. What did the man who fell among thieves do? He did nothing. Salvation has to be achieved 100% by Jesus. If we try to get our hands on it, even just a little, then that is not salvation. In terms of my salvation, if I were to say, "I did a little and Jesus did some too," that is not true salvation. When we receive salvation, it has to be the work of Jesus 100%. But if we try to add what we've done, that is not salvation, that is helping. This is the reason many people today cannot receive salvation. People want to do something for themselves like keep the law, perform good deeds, and give offerings to be saved. That's why they're unable to receive it yet.

Taking a very close look at the man who fell among thieves, we can see that he didn't do anything. That's why it is salvation. Many churches today blend and mix their own works in with salvation. That's why so many people are unable to gain the assurance of salvation. If our salvation has been achieved by Jesus dying on the cross for our sins, there is no more effort that needs to be blended in. All we need to do is simply accept what Jesus has already accomplished.

Because people who go to church today know the Bible incorrectly, they are confused in thinking they have to do something. If people feel like they have done some good, or have said many prayers, they say, "God, thank you for bestowing your grace upon me." Then when they commit sins, they say, "God, I'm a sinner." Do not be deceived. Salvation has nothing to do with our works. Saying that we have to do something is the voice of Satan. Salvation has to be 100% by Jesus.

The Things Done by the Good Samaritan

In Luke chapter 10, it was the good Samaritan who did all of the work for the man who fell among thieves. The man who fell among thieves simply laid there. The Bible says, "A certain Samaritan as he journeyed came

to where he was, saw him, and had compassion on him."
The Samaritan had the heart of wanting to save the man
who fell among thieves. And the Bible reveals the actions
the Samaritan took, one by one.

Regarding the phrase, "...went to him," who went to
him? The Samaritan went to the man who fell. Did the
Samaritan go to the man who fell, or did the man go to
the Samaritan? It was the Samaritan. The savior came
close to us. However, many people today are constantly
trying to bring themselves closer to Jesus. Jesus is the
one who needs to come close to us.

The Bible also uses the phrase, "...bound up his
wounds, pouring in oil and wine." These days, we
have good medical equipment, as well as many good
hospitals and pharmacies. A long time ago, when you
were wounded on the road, you would first get wine
poured into your wound since the wine has alcohol
(a disinfectant). Though not as effective as actual
disinfectants, wine can disinfect the wounds.

Then, you have to protect the wound. If there is a
burn, the skin is unable to fend off germs. That's why
they apply Vaseline. The Vaseline protects the body by
blocking germs from entering. Certain oils have similar
characteristics to Vaseline. After you disinfect a wound
with the alcohol, you apply oil to prevent germs from
entering the body.

However, here, the Samaritan does not pour the
wine out first, then apply the oil. The Bible says he first
poured oil onto the wound, and then wine. The order
is backwards. Oil represents the Holy Spirit, and wine

represents joy. After the Holy Spirit comes upon us, and then we are filled with the joy of living as saved people.

After the oil and wine is poured onto the wound, the Samaritan bound it so the treatments would not dry up and evaporate. Then, he put the fallen man onto his beast, brought him to an inn, and took care of him. The next day, he took out two pence and gave them to the inn keeper. "Take care of him," the Samaritan said. "Whatsoever thou spendest more, I will repay you when I get back."

The good Samaritan did ten things to save the man who fell among thieves. Did the fallen man do any of those things? Not even one. They were all done by the good Samaritan. It was the good Samaritan who saw the man who had fallen. The Samaritan had compassion on him. The Samaritan went to him. The Samaritan poured oil and wine on the wounds. The Samaritan bound them up. The Samaritan put the man who fell on his beast and took him to the inn. It was the Samaritan who took care of him and told the inn keeper to take care of him. And it was the Samaritan who told the inn keeper he would repay him for the extra expenses needed.

Lifting your hands for this work of salvation in any way, would cause more problems...the more you touch, the more problems to be had. And the more damage caused. Jesus must be the one to do it.

Man, Who Is Only Evil Continually

After Jesus finished speaking about the good Samaritan who saved the man who had fallen among thieves, he asked the lawyer a question.

"In your opinion, who was the neighbor to the man who fell among thieves?"

The lawyer replied, "The one who showed compassion on him."

Then, Jesus said, "Go, and do thou likewise."

According to the words of Jesus, if we try to act like the good Samaritan, we'll get to know clearly that we're unable to do so. If you saw a man who had been attacked by thieves, could you really do what the good Samaritan did? Can you love God with all your heart, with all your will, with all your strength, and with all your might? Can you love your neighbor as you love yourself? You absolutely cannot. You may do that briefly. However, because our hearts are drawn to the desires of the flesh, we are unable to do that at all times. We are not the savior. We are the people in need of the savior.

Many people read the Bible backwards. There are people who think they have to try hard to become like the good Samaritan. In Romans chapter 7, verse 18, Apostle Paul says, *For I know that in me (that is, in my flesh,) dwelleth no good thing...* And in Genesis chapter 6, verse 5, it says, *And God saw that the wickedness of man was great in the earth, and that every imagination of the thoughts of his heart was only evil continually.* God saw us and said that the imagination of the thoughts of our heart are only evil continually. But people don't think like that. They think, "I am evil, but I also have good," and tell themselves, "There are things that I have done well."

When I was ministering in the city of Daegu, Padong, I

once preached about how man is only evil continually. A church member who operated a pharmacy told me what she did in the past. She asked me, "Aren't these things good?" For example, she had customers who needed to purchase medicine regularly from her pharmacy. But there were times where people would not come back for prescription refills. This is because Padong was on the outskirts of the city of Daegu and many of the people who lived there were poor, so they did not have the money to maintain their prescriptions. However, if they did not take their medication regularly, their conditions would only get worse. So, this church member would often call them with the heart to give them free medicine.

She would ask them, "Ma'am, do you have your medicine?"

"No, I do not."

"Then, why are you not coming back to buy medicine?"

"I don't have money."

"You need to keep taking your medicine. If you just stop in the middle, you're going to be in big trouble."

"But I'm broke, what am I supposed to do?"

"Take the medicine for now. Later on, you can pay me back when you can afford to."

She gave away medicine like this. Only about 20% of those people paid her back, and the remaining customers never repaid her.

That sister asked me, "Wasn't giving medicine to poor people a good deed?"

I replied, "Yes, that is right. That was good of you. However, that was not true goodness."

She asked me, "Why not, Pastor?" So, I explained everything to her.

The Goodness of Man, Which Is Like a Gold-Plated Necklace

Once, I visited a church in the United States, and held a conference there. A lady who attended the church I was visiting ran an accessory shop. She gave me a handful of gold necklaces as a gift. There are many times after a flight, where I have to immediately run out of the airport and rush to the service venues. I need to go through customs very quickly to do that. Therefore, I would never carry anything in my bags that might cause an issue at customs. I thought that the gold necklaces might cause a delay at customs if I had them with me. So, I left them behind and came home.

After the conference, I boarded the airplane and arrived at Incheon International Airport, where the customs officer asked me, "Do you have anything to declare?"

I answered, "No, I do not."

Then the officer asked, "May I check your bag?"

So, I answered, "Yes, go ahead."

As soon as he opened my bag, he saw the necklaces. I didn't know what to do. I imagined the media reporting, "Pastor Ock Soo Park was caught smuggling gold necklaces." Here's what happened: right before I left America, I went to the restroom. While I was in the restroom, someone must have thought, "Oh, Pastor forgot to pack this," and put the necklaces into my bag.

So, I told the customs officer, "These are not real gold necklaces. They're just gold plated. Pure gold necklaces are very hard to come by."

The customs officer replied, "We can't tell the difference between gold-plated necklaces and real gold necklaces. You should have declared this."

I told him I was sorry and asked him if they had a knife. He said, "Yeah, we do."

So, I asked him, "Can you bring me the knife?" The customs officer brought a knife, and I told him, "Go ahead and scrape the necklace."

"Is it okay for me to scrape them? I'm not going to be responsible."

"Yes, go ahead and scrape them."

The customs officer began to scrape the necklaces with the knife. It was gold on the outside, but when he scraped it just a little, there was another metal underneath. They were not real gold necklaces. They were just plated with gold.

So, I told the sister who worked at the pharmacy, "Sister, the good that you did was just good-plated goodness. Real gold necklaces will continue to be gold, no matter how much you scrape. If some other metal appears after you scrape, it means the metal is gold-plated. It's not a pure gold necklace. You do good things, but they are only good-plated goodness. There is evil underneath it all. If it's going to be true goodness, then it should be good all the way to the end. However, we are not good. We are only good on the outside. We may be good in the eyes of other people, however, we're not that way on the inside. We're evil. God sees our hearts—the Bible says we are only evil continually. That is why we should not exert our own goodness.

Miseon, Who Received Salvation and Went to the Lord

I knew a young lady named, Miseon Nam, who passed away from tuberculosis. It really broke my heart. In the summertime, we hold summer retreats at our retreat center in the city of Gimcheon. We would usually hold three or four consecutive sessions in a season, so I spend most of my time at the retreat center during the summer.

One time, after lunch, I was playing sports with a few other pastors when a lady approached me and said, "Pastor, my relatives are here. Would you be willing to meet with them briefly?" She was asking me to preach the word to them. How could I, a pastor, refuse to do so just because I was exercising? So, I went to them. They were a mother and daughter. The daughter was a young lady named Miseon Nam. She was 22 years old. She caught tuberculosis and was taking medication for it. Afterwards, she was healed, so she stopped taking the medicine. That was the problem.

I heard that you need to take tuberculosis medication for a long period of time in order to treat it. She thought she was healed, so she stopped taking her medication. However, she relapsed not long after that. The relapsed tuberculosis bacterium developed an immunity toward her medication. No matter what she took, it was ineffective. And even though I preached the Word of God to this young lady, she didn't want to listen. She just went home the next day. It was very unfortunate.

After four months passed, I received a phone call from Miseon's mother. "Pastor, do you have time tomorrow?"

"Yes, I have an hour between three and four."

"Pastor, I will come by tomorrow."

The next day, she came with Miseon. Miseon really hated believing in Jesus. Her mother had dragged her to me.

So, I asked her, "Miseon, have you ever heard of a person who was healed of their disease through prayer?"

"What does that have to do with me?" Her reaction was so cold that I didn't know what to do. Still, I could not just fight with this young lady.

So, I asked her, "Hey Miseon, what's wrong?" She did not even have the smallest interest in spiritual life. I usually preach the word with confidence, but that day, it felt as if I was the sinner. It was so difficult to lead her to the word. Miseon just left that day, too.

Ten days later, Miseon's mother called me again, saying, "Pastor, do you have time tomorrow?"

I replied, "Yes, you can come at this time."

So, we made an appointment. I had never felt this way before, but I started getting nervous. I thought, "What if Miseon gets angry when she comes today?" Soon after, Miseon and her mother arrived. I politely said, "Miseon, have a seat here. I'll keep it short today, and I'll speak very quietly."

For this young lady to live a spiritual life, I needed to first speak to her about receiving the forgiveness of sins. I was checking her eyes, worried that she might get angry as I preached. However, she was only getting angry because she didn't know any better. That's why I felt that I should not fight with her, but treat her nicely. That's what a pastor does. So, I explained the forgiveness of sins to Miseon.

Afterwards, I asked her, "Miseon, do you believe this?"

She replied, "Yes, I believe."

Miseon said that she believed, but I couldn't believe her. I asked her mother, "Do you also believe this?"

And her mother replied, "Yes, Pastor. Our sins have been washed away."

Miseon's mother told me that they went to the hospital a few days prior. After Miseon's treatment, they were getting ready to leave the hospital, when the doctor in charge asked to speak with her mother. She told Miseon to stay in the car, and went back into the hospital to speak with the doctor.

The doctor said, "Ma'am we have to ask you to stop coming to the hospital. We have no medication here that can help Miseon. It is painful for us to act as if we are actually treating Miseon's disease. The tuberculosis bacteria in Miseon's body have developed an immunity to any medication we administer. We have no effective medicine for her. It's only harming her stomach and is not helping her at all. We're very tormented by this, so please stop coming to the hospital."

What this meant was that Miseon was going to die. So, her mother said, "Okay. I understand," and drove her car home. She told Miseon to stay in the house, and went outside for a walk by herself. In the middle of the rain, she walked around the city. She just cried and cried. "Miseon, if you leave me, how will I live?" It grew late so she wanted to go back home, but on her way home, she passed a fortuneteller who she knew very well. She approached the fortuneteller, who was stunned to see her.

"Hey, what are you doing walking around in the pouring rain?" the fortuneteller asked.

She answered, "Well, you know. Some things have happened."

She dried her hair with a towel and sat down. Miseon's mother asked the fortuneteller, "I'll do anything, if you could just tell me how I can save Miseon's life." The fortuneteller smiled and told her that there were only two ways. So, the mother asked for her to say what they were.

The fortuneteller said that she should gather a lot of money and give it as an offering. And, if Miseon were to receive a spirit and become a witch, she would be able to live. Miseon's mother had the heart, "Well, if that's what it takes, then that's what we need to do in order to save Miseon." However, on the other side of her heart, she felt differently. "I really don't want to turn my beautiful Miseon into a witch." She asked the fortuneteller for the other way.

The fortuneteller stared at Miseon's mother for a good while and opened her mouth and told her that it was to believe Jesus. The words of that fortuneteller were more effective than the words of a pastor. In this mother's heart, she thought, "That's right. We'll believe in Jesus, then." Miseon was already asleep when the mother got home, so she reached under her blanket and held Miseon's hand. She knew that Miseon didn't like her to pray, so she prayed silently, saying, "Jesus, please save Miseon's life.

The next day, Miseon's mother told Miseon, "Miseon, there is something I need to tell you."

"What is it, Mom?"

"I heard that if you gave an offering, accepted a spirit, and became a witch, you will be able to live."

"Mom, I don't want to become a witch. That's scary. I really don't want that. What else can we do?"

"I was told that if you don't want to become a witch, you have to believe in Jesus."

"I'll believe in Jesus, then."

So, that day, Miseon came to me with a different heart. I was very careful in preaching the Word of God, and Miseon received the forgiveness of sins. Miseon said, "Mom, it's weird. Pastor Park preached the word for more than an hour. And I didn't cough once the entire time." That day, the mother and daughter both received the forgiveness of sins and went home with a happy heart. They lived in a different city, so I didn't know where they were located. I only had their phone numbers.

Once, we had an event at the Choongnam University. After my lecture, I exited through the back. Miseon and her mother were there waiting for me. I was so happy to see them. Miseon's face looked very healthy.

I asked Miseon's mother, "What do you do for a living?"

She replied, "We have a lot of wealth handed down to us from our family. We just live well without increasing or decreasing our wealth."

I told her mother, "Buy Miseon lots of delicious things to eat."

"Yes, these days she's been eating so much, it's a problem."

Miseon's stomach was better because she was no longer taking the tuberculosis medicine. And she said, "Come on, Mom. I'm digesting fine. What's the problem?"

That was the last time I saw Miseon. A few months later, Miseon's mother called me on the phone, and said, "Pastor, our beautiful Miseon was called by God, and she has passed on." I was so thankful that she lived happily after receiving salvation, and then returned to the Lord's arms.

Your Excellency, the President, Who Judges Your Sins?

How did the man who fell among thieves in the Bible receive salvation? He didn't do anything at all. Jesus did everything. Jeremiah chapter 31, verse 34 says, ... *saith the Lord: for I will forgive their iniquity, and I will remember their sin no more.* Who forgives our sins? Jesus forgives our sins. God sent Jesus, and He was crucified, receiving all of the punishment for our sins. Therefore, our sins have been washed. We did not do something for it, such as good deeds. All of our good is only gold-plated goodness—they shouldn't be included. We must have Jesus do everything like the man who fell among thieves.

Both you and I have committed sins. Jesus was crucified in order to wash away our sins, and He has washed them away to perfection. He shed His blood on the cross, suffered the pain, and then washed away all our sins. We should not say that we are sinners. We have sinned, but we have been washed as white as snow through the blood of Jesus. "What can wash away my sin? Nothing but the blood of Jesus." The Bible tells us that the blood of Jesus has washed away our sins.

When I visited Ghana a few years ago, I met the president. The president told me, "I've been receiving treatment, but my sickness has only gotten worse. When I woke up this morning, it felt like I may only have five days to live."

The president was worried about sin as he stood before death, and so I asked him, "Your Excellency, how did you know you are a sinner?"

He answered, "I have committed sins, so I am a sinner, aren't I?"

I replied, "Not so." The president's eyes opened wide, and he stared at me. "In Ghana, does the person who committed a crime, judge his own sins?"

"Not at all."

"Who judges them?"

"The judge does."

"Your Excellency, have you ever seen the verdict for your sins?"

"Where is that? I'd like to see it," he answered.

I replied, "It's in the Bible. Would you like to see it?"

I opened the Bible, and read Romans chapter 3, verse 23: *For all have sinned, and come short of the glory of God;* In verse 23, it clearly says that we have committed sins, and we were sinners. However, if you look at verse 24, we are not sinners. Jesus has washed away all of our sins through His crucifixion on the cross and the redemption that is in Him. *Being justified freely by his grace through the redemption that is in Christ Jesus. (Romans 3:24)* Jesus tells us that He has justified us, without us doing anything at all.

The president said, "I am a sinner!"

So, I replied, "No, your sins were all washed away on the cross."

It's about believing this. You have to consider that all the good that you have is garbage, and you must look only to the cross of Jesus. Jesus clearly died for our sins at the cross. Our sins were finished through His crucifixion.

For I will forgive their iniquity, and I will remember their sin no more. (Jeremiah 31:34) We must not believe in our own thoughts, but believe in these words. Then we become holy and perfect. In Luke chapter 10, the man who fell among thieves did nothing at all. It was the good Samaritan who did everything. We should do nothing at all for our sins, rather, we should believe in what Jesus has done. If you believe in your heart, the Holy Spirit will work inside of you.

Chapter 3

God Who Made the New Covenant

God Who Made
the New Covenant

During this online Bible Seminar, many pastors from around the globe have attended, congratulated us, and also gave us hope. However, even more precious than this is the word that God has given us. God has expressed His heart through the Bible. If we could know the heart of God precisely, and then accept it, anyone could become happy. I am so happy that we can speak with the Bible open like this. We will read from Exodus chapter 25, verse 10:

> *And they shall make an ark of shittim wood: two cubits and a half shall be the length thereof, and a cubit and a half the breadth thereof, and a cubit and a half the*

height thereof. And thou shalt overlay it with pure gold, within and without shalt thou overlay it, and shalt make upon it a crown of gold round about. And thou shalt cast four rings of gold for it, and put them in the four corners thereof; and two rings shall be in the one side of it, and two rings in the other side of it. And thou shalt make staves of shittim wood, and overlay them with gold. And thou shalt put the staves into the rings by the sides of the ark, that the ark may be borne with them. The staves shall be in the rings of the ark: they shall not be taken from it. And thou shalt put into the ark the testimony which I shall give thee. And thou shalt make a mercy seat of pure gold: two cubits and a half shall be the length thereof, and a cubit and a half the breadth thereof. And thou shalt make two cherubims of gold, of beaten work shalt thou make them, in the two ends of the mercy seat. And make one cherub on the one end, and the other cherub on the other end: even of the mercy seat shall ye make the cherubims on the two ends thereof. And the cherubims shall stretch forth their wings on high, covering the mercy seat with their wings, and their faces shall look one to another; toward the mercy seat shall the faces of the cherubims be. And thou shalt put the mercy seat above upon the ark; and in the ark thou shalt put the testimony that I shall give thee. And there I will meet with thee, and I will commune with thee from above the mercy seat, from between the two cherubims which are upon the ark of the testimony, of all things which I will give thee in commandment unto the children of Israel. (Exodus 25:10-22)

The Curse Which Came After the Law

The Israelites came out from Egypt after living there as slaves. The Nile River of Egypt flows from south to north. The Nile River flows from inland Africa, and as it flows downward, leaves from trees and other rotten things flow down together with the river water. Sand is heavy and falls to the bottom of the river, but other bits of debris are light, so they continue to flow downstream. Then they begin to pile up towards the lower end of the river. When those things pile up higher and higher, the bottom of the river rises, and the waters of the river are no longer able to flow. As a result, the river forks to the left and to the right. This is how deltas develop, and delta land is very fertile and very good for farming.

When Joseph became the governor of Egypt, Jacob and all his children moved to Egypt. They settled in the land of Goshen, which was at the lower end of the Nile River's fertile delta land. They lived in Egypt for 430 years, but later, pharaohs who did not know Joseph reigned in Egypt. They began to enslave the descendants of Joseph, who had saved Egypt.

Then in 1491 BC, the people of Israel come out from Egypt. There is no record of this in the Bible, but it is generally understood that it happened around 1491 BC. They came out from Egypt, crossed the Red Sea, and entered the Sinai Peninsula. There, God calls Moses up to Mount Sinai. Through Moses, God told the people of Israel, "If you keep the law that I give you, you will be blessed, but if you don't keep the law, you will be cursed." Right then, the people of Israel answered that they would keep all of them. Therefore, on Mount Sinai, God recorded the Ten Commandments on two tablets of stone, and then gave them to Moses.

You shall have no other gods before me.

You shall not make idols unto yourselves.

You shall not take the Lord thy God's name in vain.

You shall remember the Sabbath to keep it holy.

Honor thy parents.

Thou shalt not murder.

Thou shalt not commit adultery.

Thou shalt not steal.

Thou shalt not give false testimony.

Thou shalt not covet.

Thus, the ten laws were recorded. So what happened when the tablets of stone, upon which the Ten Commandments were recorded, were given to Moses? While Moses was on Mount Sinai for 40 days, there was no news of him. The Israelites who were at the bottom of the mountain began to think, "There's no food and no water to drink on that mountain. How could Moses stay up there for 40 days? Moses must be dead. We should make a god who will lead us."

Aaron told them to hand over the gold necklaces, rings, and other gold jewelry—with the gold they gathered, they made a golden calf. Then Aaron proclaimed, "Now, this is the god who brought you out of Egypt." Aaron did this because he needed a focal point to gather the hearts of the people. It was God who led them. But now, they made a golden calf that was not God and began to serve that.

When Moses came down, carrying the two tablets of stone that had the Ten Commandments written on them, he saw that the people of Israel had made a golden calf. They were giving offerings to it, and they were singing and dancing in front of it. When Moses saw this, he threw down the tablets of stone he was carrying and shattered them.

There has to be a law in order for sin to exist. Every country has traffic laws. In Korea, the speed limit is usually 100 km per hour on the Gyungbu Highway. There are some sections of this highway where the limit increases to 110 km/hr. If you drive faster than the speed limit and get caught, you have to pay a fine because you have violated the traffic laws.

On the other hand, without this law, then even if you were to be travelling at 1,000 or 10,000 km/hr, it would not be a crime or violation. Before the Ten Commandments, or the law was given, not serving God would not have been a problem. However, the people of Israel promised they would keep the law that God gave them, and then they broke it. They made a golden calf, so they violated the two commandments that said, "You shall have no other gods before me," and "You shall not make idols unto yourselves."

Moses had no choice but to shatter the tablets of stone, because the people must be cursed if the tablets of stone are present. Regardless of this, 3,000 people were ultimately put to death for committing the sin of making a golden calf. After the Ten Commandments were given, curses continually came upon the people of Israel. Lying is a sin, complaining against God is a sin, stealing is a sin, and committing adultery is a sin. Many sins were established, and therefore, the people of Israel needed to be cursed.

Put the Tablets of the Ten Commandments into the Ark and Close the Lid

Today, what we must surely know is how to treat the tablets of stone with the Ten Commandments recorded on them. The Bible says that the two tablets of stone were to be placed into a box. That box is called the ark of the covenant. They made the lid for it, and they closed the ark. On the lid, there were two angels that covered the lid with their wings. Exodus chapter 25, verse 16 has recorded this: *And thou shalt put into the ark the testimony which I shall give thee.* Here, "the testimony" is referring to the tablets of stone with the Ten Commandments.

Exodus chapter 25, verse 17 says, *And thou shalt make a mercy seat of pure gold: two cubits and a half shall be the length thereof, and a cubit and a half the breadth thereof.* The mercy seat is made of pure gold, and it serves as the lid of the ark of the covenant.

There are two angels that cover the mercy seat with their wings:

And thou shalt make two cherubims of gold, of beaten work shalt thou make them, in the two ends of the mercy seat. And make one cherub on the one end, and the other cherub on the other end: even of the mercy seat shall ye make the cherubims on the two ends thereof. And the cherubims shall stretch forth their wings on high, covering the mercy seat with their wings, and their faces shall look one to another; toward the mercy seat shall the faces of the cherubims be. (Exodus 25:18-20)

The two angels covering the mercy seat are telling us, "Do not open up this lid." Why is God telling us to not open the lid? He is telling us to not look at the Ten Commandments.

In the hymnals published in Korea, the Lord's Prayer and the Apostle's Creed are printed on the front pages of the hymnal. The Ten Commandments are printed on the back pages of the hymnal. We must know what the Lord's Prayer is precisely about.

A long time ago when I used to attend a Presbyterian church, they used to end their regular services by reciting the Lord's Prayer. However, when you read what the Lord taught about prayer in the book of Matthew, He says to not do vain repetitions. This means that when people pray, they say many things that are not in their heart. That's why he taught them saying, "Pray in this manner." He did not tell them to just recite it. However, people recite it over and over.

"Our father, who art in heaven, hallowed be thy name. Thy kingdom come, thy will be done, on earth as it is in heaven. Give us this day our daily bread…" With food stockpiled at home, is asking for your daily bread a true prayer? What does "Thy will be done on earth as it is in heaven" mean? This is expressing the hope that our sins will be forgiven on earth the same way that they are in heaven. This is talking about the work of Jesus Christ being crucified to wash our sins away. Jesus has already accomplished His work. However, people do not know the meaning of this, and so they simply recite the prayer. Jesus really hates superficial prayers that are not from the heart.

Teaching the World of the Heart to Youths

I cannot overstate how important it is to properly understand the Bible. I discovered the world of the heart by reading the Bible, and I educate young people on it. There was a man named Lamech who appears in the Bible. Lamech had three sons. His first son was a rancher. The second one became the father of those who handle the harp and organ. The third one became an artificer of brass and iron.

His first son needed to be a rancher because his parents were getting old, and he needed to care for his younger siblings. He would milk the cows and sheep, and he would also eat them. He made tents out of cowhides and made clothes out of sheep's wool.

How did the second son come to handle the harp and organ? Thanks to his older brother, he had no problems with food or shelter. So, in order to find pleasure, he made musical instruments and played music.

Why did the third son become an artificer of brass and iron? He too had no problems with eating and living, and he grew sick and tired of the sound of music, so he forged sharp weapons. He would take those weapons and fight wild bears. He felt pleasure and excitement from stabbing and killing them. That's the kind of person he became.

Through this story, the Bible has precisely recorded the path by which the heart of man flows. Based on the world of the heart I discovered in the Bible, I teach the youth how to have self-control, how to think deeply, and how to have exchange. When they learn this, it really improves their personal relationships, and they're able to adjust to society very well.

A long time ago in Korea, if a family had five daughters and a son, the son would usually end up becoming an alcoholic. Because they were raised so spoiled, they were unable to learn self-control. They became accustomed to doing whatever they wanted to do. Therefore, they are unable to cope when things don't go as they wish. They end up incapable of living a normal life. As I raised my daughter and my son, I taught my children about the world of the heart when they were about seven years old. The most important thing was to instill self-control in them.

After discovering the new land of America, I heard that the settlers were very wise and healthy. However, Dr. Benjamin Spock, a pediatrician, wrote a book called, *The Commonsense Book of Baby and Child Care.* The main concept was that when a baby cries, go ahead and breastfeed it because this is the baby telling the mother he or she needs to be fed. That's why the baby is crying.

The Puritans who first came to the United States were very strict with raising their children. The early Puritan mothers would breastfeed their babies according to a schedule. They did not feed the baby just because he or she cried. Even if the babies wanted to eat, they would have to wait until it was feeding time. These babies grew up, having the ability to exercise self-control at a young age because they were raised that way. They were the ones who built America.

Later, industries grew very rapidly, and they were even able to complete the Empire State Building in 13 months. I've built churches before, and it takes about a month to build one floor. However, they completed a 102-story building in 13 months. The workers were able to complete the building in a very short timeframe. This was possible because the American people were very advanced and strong in regard to self-control.

Many people have read the books written by Dr. Benjamin Spock, and there have been many who've said, "No, this can't be. What this book is teaching is wrong." However, many mothers in America felt that Dr. Spock had to be right since he was a pediatrician. Therefore, they broke the habit of feeding based on a schedule and started to breastfeed their babies whenever the baby cried. From then on, it significantly decreased the self-control in children and brought about many problems in American society.

When I raised my children, I wanted to nurture self-control in them. When my kids asked me to buy something for them, if they asked, "Dad, can we have some candy?" I would buy them candy. When they would say, "Dad, we want ice cream," I would buy them ice cream. It made me happy to see my children happy from eating candy or ice cream. However, I needed to nurture self-control in them. And that is why, if they made ten requests, I would only listen to them seven times, and deny them three times.

So they would ask me, "Dad, can we have some ice cream?"

I would answer, "No."

They would plead, "Dad?"

But then I'd reply, "Dad said no."

"But Dad?"

"Dad said no!"

My children were so young at the time and they could not overpower me since I was an adult. I taught self-control to my children, who were kids that wanted ice cream. Even though they would cry and press me, it did not work. My children learned to have self-control, and in turn, were very different from other kids.

My son attended high school in America. His school was far from where he stayed, and in the United States, you can get your driver's license when you're 16. So, I bought him a car, the cheapest car in America at the time, a Ford Escort. My son said that he was so thankful. Many other international students had wealthy fathers and drove nice cars like BMWs.

Those students would also go skiing on Saturdays. The ski resorts were only about 100 to 200 kilometers away. Because the kids had cars, they would go skiing and had lots of fun. They would leave on Saturday, ski through Sunday, and then return to school on Monday. They told my son, "Hey, we went skiing this week, and it was so fun. You should come with us." My son also wanted to go, but he could not.

He lived in the church, and needed to clean and do other work for them. His friends went skiing on Sundays, and my son had to attend church services. Therefore, he was unable to go. Because the kids had so much fun skiing, they would leave on Saturday and return on Monday. The next time, they left on a Saturday and returned on a Tuesday. Then, they would return on a Wednesday. Since the students are not restricted from doing anything they wanted, they were able to do whatever they wanted. What do you think the result of that was? On the day of their high school graduation, they received envelopes. However, the envelopes that the students who went skiing received were empty, with no diplomas.

If you learn self-control, little by little, from a young age, then even after you are grown, you can have self-control from the things that you want to do. Because I'm a pastor, I read the Bible a lot. For the most part, the Bible talks about the world of the heart. I teach people the world of the heart that I learned from the Bible. I teach the students that come to my church how to have self-control and how to think.

My son is almost fifty years old now, and whenever I have spoken to him, he has never once told me no. My grandchildren learned that from their father, and they listen to their father as well. How is it that they have become people capable to listening to the words of others? It is because they have learned self-control. And that was possible because the opportunity for my kids to have self-control was given to them from a young age. Self-control is not taught in a complicated way. All you have to do is have your children control themselves a few times when they ask for ice cream. At the age of six or seven, that is not that hard to do. When self-control is formed, then even at the age of 20 or 30, they have the strength to have self-control.

What the young people need to learn next is deep thinking. Deep thinking is also very simple to learn. It's not thinking about something in a complicated way. When there is a certain problem, think about it from the first level of thought. Then place that thought aside and think about it from another angle. The second level of that thought is much better than the first level. Then after that, just think about it again from a third level. Because people do not like to think, people oftentimes decide things based on their first level of thought. When a child is young, teach them how to think deeply, and lead them to think at the first, second, and third levels of thought. The second level of thinking is much better than the first level. And the third level of thinking is even better than the second level.

In Korea, today, most couples only have one child. This is the wrong choice. Oftentimes, they only have one child because they want to live comfortably, but that is actually not true. A child who is alone will often exert his or her own wants, and they do not listen to their parents. This causes the parents lots of grief. The members of our churches usually have three or four children. When a woman has a child, her name becomes, "mother." There is a huge difference between a woman and a mother. If a woman has five children, no matter how wicked that woman may have been, she changes into a saint.

My daughter-in-law had a son, then a daughter, and then her third child was a son. We call the third child, "P-I-G" as a nickname. I could see that of my three grandchildren, my daughter-in-law really loves the third one. The more children a mother has, the greater the love grows in her heart, and she cherishes her children. Therefore, no matter how wicked a woman may have been, when she has five children, she pretty much becomes a saint. It is better to have two children than one. Three is better than two, and four is better than three. When the children do something wrong, most parents will tell them not to do it again, and just pass everything by. However, older brothers are not that way. My eldest grandson learned wrestling at his school. When his little brother does not listen, he puts a lock on him with his arms and pushes him down. Then his little brother would shout, "I'm really sorry. I won't do that again!" That is how the older brother takes care of his younger brother. That is how they get along with one another, and that's why the children from families that have many siblings have really good personal relationships.

The Reason God Gave the Law to Man

God gave man the Ten Commandments. The reason God made the law was very simple. We must first know sin in order to receive the forgiveness of sins. God made the law so that people would realize what sin is. When the laws, "Do not steal. Do not commit adultery," are made, then stealing and committing adultery become sins. That is how people realize that they have committed sins. The law was made because sin was present. The law didn't come first and then sin came about. But sin existed, that's why the law was made. Because there were people who steal, a law that says, "Do not steal," had to be made. Because there were people who lied, the law that says, "Do not lie," was made.

Around the world, laws are made to prevent people from sinning. However, God gave man His law in order for all mankind to realize their sins. The reason for this is that although people commit sins, they would not realize they were sinners without the law. The reason God gave people the Ten Commandments was not for them to be blessed and live well by successfully keeping the Ten Commandments. Instead, the law was given so people would discover that they were sinners. And it was so that people would come before Jesus in order to have their sins washed away and receive the forgiveness of sins.

The People Who Opened Up the Lid of the Ark and Looked In

The law was given to the people of Israel, and the curse followed them whenever a sin was committed. However, God did not want the people to look at the Ten Commandments. God did not want to meet with man through the law. This was because the people would have to be cursed and destroyed if they broke the law. That's why God placed the tablets of stone containing the inscribed Ten Commandments inside of the ark. Then God ordered the lid closed. That lid was called the mercy seat, in other words, the place where mercy is given.

Putting the Ten Commandments into the ark and closing the lid is saying, "Do not look at this." It means that all you need to do is realize you're a sinner. God put the Ten Commandments inside of the ark so people would not be able to look at it. Then God ordered the lid closed so that people would not freely open it up. And on top of it all, there are two angels covering the lid with their wings.

In the Bible, a priest named Eli appears. He was very evil. He did not train other priests to follow in his footsteps. Therefore, his two sons Hophni and Phinehas worked as priests. Those two men did many evil deeds in the holy place. They slept with the women who helped with the offerings. They also demanded meat before the offerings were given. They completely despised the offerings that were to be given to God.

Then, a war broke out between Israel and the Philistines. When Israel was getting pushed around, they brought out the ark of the covenant onto the battlefield. When the ark came onto the battlefield of Israel, the soldiers of Israel roared. The Philistines were shocked, and said, "Why are the Israelites shouting so loudly?" They heard that the ark of the covenant had been brought out, and they trembled. They said, "Their God is so fierce, and He smote the people of Egypt. Still, we should go out and fight. If we lose, we'll be servants to the people of Israel." The Philistines went out and fought, and Israel lost the war. Both of Eli's sons died, and Israel lost the ark of the covenant. The ark remained in the land of the Philistines for seven months. Wherever the ark went, curses came about, so the Philistines returned it to Israel. When the ark was returned, Eli's two sons had already died, and there were no priests in Israel. They did not know what to do with the ark. Therefore, there were people who thought, "What's inside of this? Shall we look inside?" They opened the lid of the ark of the covenant and many people died: *And he smote the men of Bethshemesh, because they had looked into the ark of the LORD, even he smote of the people fifty thousand and threescore and ten men: and the people lamented, because the LORD had smitten many of the people with a great slaughter. (1 Samuel 6:19)*

Not by the Law, but a New Law

God did not want us to look at the Ten Commandments. If He wanted us to look at the law, He would have told us to look at them every day. If God deals with us according to the law, then we will all have to be cursed and destroyed. That's why God made a new law that is not the Ten Commandments. In Jeremiah chapter 31, verse 31, it says, *Behold, the days come, saith the Lord, that I will make a new covenant with the house of Israel, and with the house of Judah.* Why did God make a new covenant? Because under the law, which was the first covenant, everyone had to be cursed. With the first covenant, if you kept every law, then you would be blessed. However, if you did not keep them all, you were cursed. When God said, "If you keep the law, you are blessed, but if you do not keep the law, you will be cursed," the people of Israel should have said, "God, we cannot keep the law. We have so many sins, so please do not do this." However, they swore, "Yes, Lord, we will keep all of them." Therefore, the law was called a covenant, and therefore, the ark is also known as the ark of the covenant.

God does not want us to look at the Ten Commandments. Every time we look at the law, our sins will be exposed, and it will ruin our relationship with God. That's why God paved a way for the people, who have realized their sins through the law, to come to Jesus and receive the forgiveness of sins. The lid that covered the ark which contained the stone tablets engraved with the Ten Commandments, was called, "The mercy seat." This is the place where mercy is given. God was telling us, "Let us close the lid and speak in the presence of grace."

And so, God made a new law:

Behold, the days come, saith the Lord, that I will make a new covenant with the house of Israel, and with the house of Judah: Not according to the covenant that I made with their fathers in the day that I took them by the hand to bring them out of the land of Egypt; which my covenant they brake, although I was an husband unto them, saith the Lord: (Jeremiah 31:31-32)

The people of Israel continued to break the law, which was the first covenant they promised to keep well, and under the agreement of that covenant, they could only be cursed. And for that reason, God said that the days when He would establish a new covenant were coming. God was saying that it would change into a new covenant.

Let us look at Jeremiah chapter 31, verse 33: *But this shall be the covenant that I will make with the house of Israel; After those days, saith the Lord, I will put my law in their inward parts, and write it in their hearts; and will be their God, and they shall be my people.*

And now, verse 34: *And they shall teach no more every man his neighbour, and every man his brother, saying, Know the Lord: for they shall all know me, from the least of them unto the greatest of them, saith the Lord: for I will forgive their iniquity, and I will remember their sin no more.*

What is mentioned in the second half of verse 34 is extremely important. It reads, "For I will forgive their iniquity, and I will remember their sin no more." With the first covenant, we can be blessed if we keep the law, but we will be cursed if we can't. Therefore, we would receive things depending on our performance.

However, because everyone of us has broken the laws, every one of us must be cursed and destroyed under that covenant. The new covenant that God established was completely different. God said, "For I will forgive their iniquity, and I will remember their sin no more." With the first covenant, our blessings or our curse were decided by our works. However, the second covenant has absolutely nothing to do with how well or poorly we do. God forgave our sins. Through God's working He established a law to bless us. People know the first law, the Ten Commandments, very well. However, they don't fully know the second covenant. That's why they remain in sin.

Jesus, Who Wrote with His Finger

In John chapter 8, there is a story of the woman who was taken in the act of committing adultery. This woman was caught in the act. The Pharisees and scribes brought her to Jesus and asked Him, "This woman was caught in the act of adultery. In the law, Moses commanded that such a woman should be stoned. But what do you say?" Right then, Jesus wrote on the ground with His finger. Why did He write? Because God wrote the first covenant with His finger.

In the Bible, it says that when God wrote on the tablets of stone, He wrote with His finger. And when the second covenant was being recorded, Jesus, who is God, wrote on the ground with His finger. The ground represents the heart of man. Therefore, Jesus recorded the new covenant in our hearts. *But this shall be the covenant that I will make with the house of Israel; After those days, saith the Lord, I will put my law in their inward parts, and write it in their hearts; and will be their God, and they shall be my people. (Jeremiah 31:33)* What is the content of the new covenant? As stated in verse 34, the new covenant reads: *For I will forgive their iniquity, and I will remember their sin no more.*

If the woman caught in adultery was judged according to the law of Moses, she should be stoned to death. Again, the scribes and Pharisees brought this woman before Jesus and asked Him, "This woman was caught in the act of adultery. In the law, Moses commanded that such a woman should be stoned. But master, what do you say?"

How should Jesus answer them? First, there needs to be a law that judges her. The first covenant, which is the law, established the sin of adultery. Then, Jesus established the new covenant: "For I will forgive their iniquity, and I will remember their sin no more." This is the law Jesus established. And in John chapter 8, Jesus wrote on the ground with His finger, twice. God also recorded the Ten Commandments twice. The first time was on the tablets of stone, which were shattered by Moses. God wrote them again a second time. That's why, when the new covenant was being recorded, Jesus wrote on the ground twice.

Now there are two laws. This woman needs to be stoned to death when judged by the first law. But Jesus judged her according to the new law. Jesus looked at this woman and said, "Neither do I condemn you. Go and sin no more." How amazing is this? God promised that He would establish a new covenant. Through God sending Jesus to this earth to die on the cross, He washed all of our sins as white as snow. If that is the case, then what should we do? All we have to do is believe that Jesus has washed away all of our sins on the cross.

Even now, if you follow the law, you can only be cursed. There is no need for you to follow the law. "I do not like the law. I need the new covenant you have given, God." That is how you should think. This is what God is telling us. According to the new covenant, Jesus was crucified, receiving all the punishment we should have received. By doing that, He washed away all of our sins. The sad thing is that so many people today, pray, "Lord, I'm a sinner. Please forgive me." This is because they do not believe the words written in the Bible.

When You Open the Words of the Bible, Any Problem Can Be Resolved

This happened during the Christmas Cantata tour in Korea a few years ago. We had a performance scheduled for the city of Jinju, so I got in my car and drove to Jinju in the morning. The performance usually takes place in the evening, so in the morning time, I have Bible studies with the pastors from the surrounding area. In the afternoon, I would have Bible studies with the pastors' wives. That afternoon, while having a Bible study with the pastors' wives, I was very tired and extremely sleepy. So, I told Pastor Youngjoo Park, who came with me, "Let me sleep for a little while," and asked him to preach instead. Then I leaned my head against the wall and fell asleep.

Pastor Youngjoo Park is my nephew, and he was a missionary in America. However, he had many difficulties, so I called him back to Korea. I told him, "Youngjoo, I'd like you to come and drive for me. And at the same time, it would be good for you to learn faith." We would have prayer meetings in my car, and I would have fellowship with many people over the phone. At the time, I felt it would be good to have a pastor drive my car. Pastor Youngjoo Park had difficulties in his ministry at the time, so I called him in. But as Pastor Youngjoo Park stayed with me, where I worked, he saw something amazing. He saw many brothers and sisters come with their problems, but once the Bible was opened, all their problems were resolved. As he consistently saw this happening up close, he began to have faith to believe in the Word of God. That day, I was tired and wanted to close my eyes for a little bit, but I heard what Pastor Youngjoo Park was saying. I was completely shocked. He was preaching the word with God's heart. Afterwards, Pastor Youngjoo Park was sent to a new church, and has been doing the works of the gospel, amazingly.

After the Christmas Cantata performance in Jinju ended that evening, I was scheduled to spend the night at the Good News Jinju Church. However, the brothers and sisters of the Hapcheon church asked me, "Pastor, please visit the Hapcheon church just one time." I thought this would be my only chance to do just that, so I went to the Good News Hapcheon Church. After the performance wrapped up, we arrived at the Good News Hapcheon Church around midnight. Because I had come, many brothers and sisters gathered at the church. So, I shared the words of the Bible with them way past midnight.

When I finished speaking, one sister approached me and said, "Pastor, I cannot live with my husband anymore. We've been married for 23 years. My husband was fine for the first three years, but after that, he drinks every day. Even now, he drinks soju every day."

When this sister came home from work, she would see empty bottles spread out all over the floors in every room. It was so painful for her to clean them up. She said, "Pastor, I can't live like this anymore," and started to cry. I told her to stop crying and to bring her husband to see me the next morning. The next day, she came with her husband. After the morning service, I sat face to face with him, and I read one Bible verse to him: *For by one offering he hath perfected for ever them that are sanctified. (Hebrews 10:14)*

It is not that we became holy, but Jesus gave His body to make us holy, and in addition to that, the Bible says that He perfected us forever. I told the woman's husband to read the verse, "For by one offering he hath perfected for ever them that are sanctified."

After he read it, I asked him, "In the Bible, God says that He has perfected us forever. Then, are you perfect?"

He answered, "I'm not perfect. I drink every day. How could I be perfect?"

I spoke to him again, saying, "Brother, don't look at your circumstances. Look at the heart of God. Brother, you say that you're not perfect, but the Bible says that you've been perfected forever. So, which one is right? Are you right, or are the words of the Bible right?"

He replied, "The words of the Bible are right."

"Then, you are perfect, right?"

"No, I'm not perfect."

"No, look. The Bible says that you have been perfected forever. Believe these words. In these words, 'he' is referring to Jesus. Jesus gave His body as an offering and was crucified on the cross. That's when all of our sins were washed away, forever. That's why He says we are perfected forever. Do you understand?"

"Yes, I understand."

"Then, are you perfect?"

"I am not perfect." The two of us sat and argued for a long while. After 30 minutes, the brother finally admitted that he was perfect.

So, I asked, "Brother, are you really perfect?"

"Yes, God says that I am perfect. The Word of God is right."

"But you drink."

"Still, if God says that I'm perfect, then I'm perfect. Am I not?"

"Brother, you're a drunk, but you're perfect?"

He answered, "Yes, God says that I'm perfect. So, even though I drink and lived an evil life, my sins have been washed by the blood of Jesus. If God says that He has perfected me, then I am perfect."

This man drank soju every day. Soju is a very strong liquor, so people usually drink it out of small shot glasses. When this brother would wake up, he would get two bottles of soju, pour them into a bowl, and chug everything. Then, he would begin his day. One time, his wife got so angry, she purchased four two-liter bottles of soju. She carried two bottles in each hand, and brought them home. Her husband saw this and was shocked.

He asked her, "Are you telling me to drink all of this and die?"

She replied, "That's right. I wish you were dead."

Even so, he could not help but drink. Even though he tried to quit, it was so painful that he had no choice but to drink again. His wife was unable to live with him because he was always drunk. She was unable to have conversations with him or do anything with him. But amazingly, this brother believed the words of the Bible.

Do you know what happened? The following day, he no longer thought about drinking. He was a person who used to go crazy if he didn't drink. The word entered his heart and cast out all the thoughts of wanting to drink. I told him to enroll in our theology school. Now, he is ministering in a city called, Gyeongnam Jinyoung. It is very graceful. Even though it's a small church, he and his wife are very happy. He didn't change through his own determination. God works inside of us when we accept His word in our heart.

The People Who Fight Against God

This is what people say: "I'm a sinner because I've committed sins." However, God says, "No, your sins have been washed away. My Son, Jesus, was crucified for your sins, and He received all the punishment for your sins. Your sins do not remain." God and man argue.

God says, "You are justified. You are holy."

"No, I'm a sinner."

There is no end to this. That is how it goes, and then one day man believes the Word of God. "Even though I committed sins, and even though I am evil, God says that I am justified. And if God says that I am justified, it means I am righteous. Would God say that we are justified because He doesn't know that we've committed sins? Would God not know that people have stolen or lied, and He calls them justified?" I committed lots of theft. I told many lies and committed many sins. However, the punishment for those sins ended on the cross.

God sees us as perfect. But Satan says, "You're not perfect. You're a sinner." And Satan continually tries to bind us as sinners. So many people today listen to the voice of Satan. You have no idea how many people say they are sinners, even though they claim to believe in Jesus. In Hebrews chapter 10, verse 14, it says, *For by one offering he hath perfected for ever them that are sanctified.* We commit sins, and even after we believe in Jesus, we still commit sins. And that is why people say they are sinners. However, that's not what the Bible says. It says that one offering washed our sins away forever.

The Eternal Redemption Obtained in Eternal Heaven

Let us talk about this in greater detail. In Hebrews chapter 9, verse 11, it says, *But Christ being come an high priest of good things to come, by a greater and more perfect tabernacle, not made with hands, that is to say, not of this building.*

There is the temple in heaven. Moses modeled the tabernacle after the temple in heaven. Later on, Solomon built the temple. Because this earth is a realm of time, the sin offerings given at the temple on earth are limited by time when it comes to the washing away of sins. Those offerings could only wash away the sins already committed. They could not wash away sins committed in the future. That's why if you commit sins after you have your sins washed away, you become a sinner again. So, naturally, they killed lambs every day to wash away sins during the time of the Old Testament.

The blood Jesus shed on the cross was not put upon the horns of the altar on earth—He took His blood to heaven and put it on the altar in heaven. That's what Hebrews chapter 9, verse 11 is telling us: "But Christ being come an high priest of good things to come, by a greater and more perfect tabernacle, not made with hands, that is to say, not of this building." The greater and more perfect tabernacle that is not made with hands is referring to the temple in heaven. The temple on earth was made by the hands of man. But the temple in heaven was not made by the hands of man.

Neither by the blood of goats and calves, but by his own blood... After that what does it say? ...*He entered in once into the holy place, having obtained eternal redemption for us. (Hebrews 9:12)* In heaven, everything is eternal. We cannot go to heaven with this body of ours. We must receive a new body, which will not die or become corrupted. The washing away of sins in eternal heaven is also eternal. Even though Jesus was crucified and died on this earth, He sprinkled His blood at the temple in heaven.

And every priest standeth daily ministering and offering oftentimes the same sacrifices, which can never take away sins. (Hebrews 10:11) This is talking about the offerings given at the temple on earth. This offering could only wash away the sins that have already been committed. It could not wash away sins at any time. *But this man, after he had offered one sacrifice for sins for ever, sat down on the right hand of God; From henceforth expecting till his enemies be made his footstool. (Hebrews 10:12-13)*

Jesus gave the eternal offering. That is why our sins have been washed away forever:

For by one offering he hath perfected for ever them that are sanctified. Whereof the Holy Ghost also is a witness to us: for after that he had said before, this is the covenant that I will make with them after those days, saith the Lord, I will put my laws into their hearts, and in their minds will I write them; And their sins and iniquities will I remember no more. Now where remission of these is, there is no more offering for sin. (Hebrews 10:14-18)

All sins have been washed away forever—that's why there are no sins for us to give offerings for anymore.

The Law of Sin and Death and the Law of the Spirit of Life

God does not want us to be looking at the Ten Commandments, the law. It says this in Romans chapter 8, verses 1 and 2: *There is therefore now no condemnation to them which are in Christ Jesus, who walk not after the flesh, but after the Spirit. For the law of the Spirit of life in Christ Jesus hath made me free from the law of sin and death.*

Here, the law of sin and death is the law. If you commit sins, the law condemns those sins, and the result is death. The law of the Spirit of life refers to the new covenant that Jesus established. Under this law, we will not receive things based on what we have done—we will receive things according to what Jesus has done.

In the past, elementary schools would have field days in the fall. First-graders would come with their fathers. They would be put on one team and have foot races. A certain father was running with his son and his son could not keep up, so they were about to finish in last place. However, he suddenly picked up his son, ran the race, and won first place. The son did not perform well—the father did.

The first law (the law of Moses) dictates that we receive according to how we've done. But in the second law, we receive according to what Jesus has done. Therefore, Jesus Christ's death on the cross becomes ours. When Jesus died on the cross, all of our sins had already been washed away. That is what we accept by faith. Jesus washed away all of our sins at the cross and it says that He has perfected us forever. Hebrews is telling us about this clearly and in great detail. Your sins have all been ended at the cross. Your sins do not remain. Jesus has received all the punishment for sin. Therefore, He has made us holy and righteous. Let us believe in the cross of Jesus. I praise God with a hallelujah.

Chapter 4

Led by the Law of Spirit of Life

Led by the Law of Spirit of Life

I cannot express how thankful I am that we are able to speak together with the Word of God open before us. God made the heart inside of man. When we accept the heart of God into ours, and when we become one in heart with God, then His heart flows into us. And it is so amazing that His heart leads our lives to be like His.

Even though we are reading the same Bible, it looks completely different when we read it with the heart of God. On the other hand, when we are led by Satan, like Judas Iscariot, then it doesn't matter if we're disciples of Jesus—we change into people who can betray Jesus. Let us read from Levtitus chpater 16, verse 11.

And Aaron shall bring the bullock of the sin offering, which is for himself, and shall make an atonement for himself, and for his house, and shall kill the bullock of the sin offering which is for himself: And he shall take a censer full of burning coals of fire from off the altar before the Lord, and his hands full of sweet incense beaten small, and bring it within the vail: And he shall put the incense upon the fire before the Lord, that the cloud of the incense may cover the mercy seat that is upon the testimony, that he die not: And he shall take of the blood of the bullock, and sprinkle it with his finger upon the mercy seat eastward; and before the mercy seat shall he sprinkle of the blood with his finger seven times. Then shall he kill the goat of the sin offering, that is for the people, and bring his blood within the vail, and do with that blood as he did with the blood of the bullock, and sprinkle it upon the mercy seat, and before the mercy seat: And he shall make an atonement for the holy place, because of the uncleanness of the children of Israel, and because of their transgressions in all their sins: and so shall he do for the tabernacle of the congregation, that remaineth among them in the midst of their uncleanness. And there shall be no man in the tabernacle of the congregation when he goeth in to make an atonement in the holy place, until he come out, and have made an atonement for himself, and for his household, and for all the congregation of Israel. And he shall go out unto the altar that is before the Lord, and make an atonement for it; and shall take of the blood of the bullock, and of the blood of the goat, and

put it upon the horns of the altar round about. And he
shall sprinkle of the blood upon it with his finger seven
times, and cleanse it, and hallow it from the uncleanness
of the children of Israel. (Leviticus 16:11-19)

We're Not Sinners—Our Sins Have Been Washed Away

After I received the forgiveness of sins by the blood of Jesus in 1962, I began to read the Bible. At that time, I was 18 years old. As I read the Bible, the structure of the Bible began to form in my heart, and word by word, the Bible began to change my life amazingly.

I attended church from a young age. Immediately after the Korean War was over, Korea was extremely poor, and a lot of people went hungry. I ate poorly as well when I was young. When I look at myself when I was small, because I only ate things that had no nutrients, my belly bulged out, but my legs and arms were very thin. As I grew older, I started stealing. When I hung out with my friends and it would get dark, I would steal apples and persimmons from people's farms. I stole things very often.

Back then, I attended every early morning prayer service, and I attended all the prayer meetings at the church. I would pray and sincerely ask for forgiveness of all the sins I committed the day before. And then I prayed that I would not commit sins that day. However, after I ate dinner, I would sit at the house where my friends and I hung out. As I lived that way, one day, I began to realize that my sins had been washed as white as snow by the blood of Jesus. I said that I was a sinner whenever I came before God, but God told me that He made me righteous. He said that He remembers my sins no more. From then on, my life started to change as I began to read the Bible.

Then, when I went to church and listened to the pastor's sermon, he said that we were sinners even though our sins have been clearly washed by the blood of Jesus. I thought, "No, our sins have been washed clean." I told the youths that were with me that they needed to receive the forgiveness of sins. After about a month of doing that, the church began to ostracize me. I was labeled a problematic child.

Once, I told my sister sincerely that my sins had been washed away. My sister replied, "Ock Soo, how did this happen to you? If you have faith, you're supposed to become humble. The riper the fruit becomes, the lower the branch sags down. The pastor of our church says he's a sinner. The elder says he's a sinner. It's so arrogant of you to say that your sins have been washed away. That makes no sense. How did this happen to you?" There was nothing I could say. However, according to the Bible, it was true that my sins have been washed away.

When You Realize You Are a Sinner, the Role of the Law Is Finished

God did not want to have exchange with us with the Ten Commandments standing in between. We had to be cursed and destroyed because we committed so many sins and there is no mercy in the law. That is why God established a new covenant. Romans chapter 3, verse 19 tells us the purpose of the law: *Now we know that what things soever the law saith, it saith to them who are under the law: that every mouth may be stopped, and all the world may become guilty before God.*

Like I mentioned earlier, sin existed before the law was established. Because there were people who committed adultery, a law was formed that says, "Do not commit adultery." Because there are people who steal, that's why there is a law that says, "Do not steal." Because there are people who lie, a law was formed that commanded, "Do not lie." If there was no one in the world who committed adultery, then why would there be a law that says, "Do not commit adultery?" If a person was told not to lie, that means that person has lied.

"Don't lie."

"What are you talking about? When did I lie?"

That is what people would say. However, why did God tell us to not commit adultery and steal? It is because man has already committed those sins. If a person who has committed sins, no longer commits a single sin from that point on, is he or she no longer a sinner? Even if he does not sin from that point on, he is still a sinner who has committed sins. That is why every person who tries to meet God through the law has to be cursed and destroyed. *Therefore, by the deeds of the law there shall no flesh be justified in his sight: for by the law is the knowledge of sin. (Romans 3:20)*

No flesh can be justified by the deeds of the law. No matter how well you may keep the law from now on, the fact that you committed sins renders the effort meaningless. God gave us the law to make us realize that we are sinners. God gave us the law with the sole purpose of making us realize sins. Keeping the law well will not justify a person. The purpose of the law has been achieved if it has made you realize you're a sinner. That's why it was placed inside of the ark, and why the ark was covered with a lid (so that it can never be looked at again).

God is telling the law, "Good, you are done. You stay in there." What God sincerely wants is not to meet with us through the law. God does not want to have the law laid down before us, checking to see if we did well or poorly. If we realize that we are sinners through the law, the only thing that can take care of our sins is the blood of Jesus Christ.

God did not want a man who has already realized that he is sinner to look at the law anymore. God is telling us, "You should not look at this. The more you look at it, the more of a sinner you will become. You will become distant from me. Now, look at the blood of Jesus at the cross." God placed the tablets of stone containing the Ten Commandments inside of the ark and had the mercy seat cover it. There, two angels cover the lid with their wings. In the book of Ezekiel (Old Testament) chapter 28, verse 14 it says, *Thou art the anointed cherub that covereth.* This verse is referring to the angels whose wings have covered the mercy seat so that the lid of the ark would not be opened. God gave this task to His most capable angels.

The Pastors Who Teach the Law Because They Do Not Know the Bible Very Well

God does not want to meet with us through the law. He washed away all of our sins by the blood of Jesus. He has even said that He will write the new law in our hearts and record them in our thoughts. Romans chapter 8, verse 1 says, *Therefore there is now no more condemnation to those who are in Christ Jesus."* In verse 2, it says, *"For the law of the Spirit of life in Christ Jesus hath made me free from the law of sin and death.* The law is the law of sin and death. The day the law was brought down, 3,000 people were executed. Then the people of Israel continued to violate the law, and many were put to death. The closer you come to the law; your souls die.

The sad thing is that the pastors of many churches today are teaching the law. It breaks my heart. God closed the lid of the ark so that people would not look at the law. "Don't ever look at this again. If you look at it, you will die. You'll be destroyed. The reason I gave you the law was for the knowledge of sin. If you realized your sin, then look at the blood that Jesus shed on the cross. You have to receive the forgiveness of sins there." Because the pastors of many churches do not know the Bible very well, they teach the law. The church members only know to say that they are sinners. This is something so heartbreaking.

If Jesus Works, Your Spinal Infection Is Nothing

Once after finishing a conference in Ulsan, I got in my

car and left for Seoul after 10 pm. When I calculated the time, I was set to arrive in Seoul around 2 in the morning. It's not enough time for me to sleep, so I felt that I should sleep somewhere along the way. There are many Good News Mission churches all over Korea, and any one of them would let me sleep there. I called the pastor of the Good News Daegu Church which was the closest to the highway. The pastor told me that I could spend the night at his church, but while I was talking with the people in the car, we ended up driving past Daegu. I said, "Uh oh, I'm sorry about that." The next closest church was in Gumi, so I called the pastor of the Good News Gumi Church, and we ended up sleeping at that church.

I wanted to wake up at 4 in the morning, get dressed, and quietly leave. But when I opened the door to my room, somebody was standing outside, waiting for me. I was startled. It was the pastor of the Gumi Church. He said to me, "Pastor, could you please preach at the early morning prayer service before you go?" Basically, he was asking me to pay for the night. I could not refuse him, so I preached the sermon for their early morning service.

While I was in the middle of preaching, I saw a girl sitting in a wheelchair underneath the clock at the back of the chapel. After the service was over, I approached her. "Everyone is sitting in a chair, why are you sitting in a wheelchair? Is it fun sitting in one of those?" I said, joking with her. The girl's name was Soohyun Choi. She told me she was 17 years old, and a senior in high school. She told me about herself. One day, she had lost feeling in her legs, so she cried out to her mother, "Mom, I can't feel anything in my legs."

"Really? You should be okay."

At first, the loss of feeling started in her legs. However, it began to move up higher and higher, until she had no feeling in her stomach. She went to the hospital, and they examined her. They diagnosed her with a spinal infection, and that her nerves were dead. Later on, she was unable to urinate or defecate on her own, and things became very difficult. The doctor said that she would die soon.

The entire Gumi Church prayed for this girl. She wanted to receive prayer from me, but because she was unable to urinate or defecate freely, she could not travel by car to come to see me in Seoul. So, the church prayed for her about this. "God, please allow Pastor Ock Soo Park to visit Gumi."

That night, I was not planning to go to Gumi, but because of their prayer, I ended up there. After the pastor of the Gumi church answered my phone call and invited me to come, he called Soohyun Choi's father. He said, "Pastor Ock Soo Park will be spending the night at our church. I will hold him here, so bring your daughter, Soohyun, to church for the early morning service tomorrow." That was how I met Soohyun. She was 17 years old, and she was a flowery young girl who was dying. If Jesus saw Soohyun, I felt that He would not take this flowering young life away.

In the very last part of the book of Matthew, it says that Jesus will always be with us, even until the end of the world. According to those words, it is true that Jesus is with me. And it is also true that Jesus is with

Soohyun. There is nothing I can do for Soohyun, but if Jesus is here, then her spinal infection is no problem at all. So, I put off returning to Seoul for a short while, and I spared some time to speak with Soohyun. Jesus is with us, and He wants to heal Soohyun. However, the issue is that Soohyun's heart and Jesus' heart must become one. Soohyun should also be able to have the heart, "Ah, Jesus wants to heal me. Then, He will heal me." That is when she becomes one in heart with Jesus. I know for a fact that when the words of the Bible connect with our hearts, God does amazing work inside of us.

I explained this to Soohyun, saying, "Soohyun, listen to what I'm going to tell you." Electricity will work as long the electrical lines are connected. You don't need to do anything else. You don't need to run the washing machine. If the electricity enters, it will run the motor inside the washing machine. If the motor runs, then the laundry will automatically be done. The washing machine will work if the electricity enters. If you unplug the electricity while the washing machine is running, the washing machine will say, 'I'm not going to work anymore,' and it will just stop.

Electricity flows through electrical lines. The power of Jesus flows from heart to heart. When the heart of Jesus and our hearts become one, then Jesus works. When the heart of Jesus and our hearts flow together, then the peace inside of Jesus flows inside of us. The holiness inside of Jesus flows into us; the love of Jesus comes to us; and everything inside of Jesus begins to live and work in us. That is why we don't need to stop committing sins, do good deeds, and work hard in order to serve God. It is

Jesus who has to work inside of us.

No matter how hard the washing machine tries, it cannot do any work without electricity. In addition to that, if you remove the electricity, the hard-working washing machine will stop right away. On the other hand, no matter how still the washing machine is, it will start to work once electricity comes in again. In order for Jesus to work in us, the heart of Jesus must first enter. When we receive the forgiveness of sins and have the heart that Jesus will work in our hearts, that's when Jesus enters our hearts. From then on, all the problems that arise are not our problems, but Jesus' problems.

It is impossible for the washing machine not to work when the electricity comes in. It might be possible if the washing machine was broken, but a normal washing machine will work once the electricity enters in. If the electricity is connected, your lights will turn on, your TV will work, and your refrigerator will create cold air. Household appliances are designed to work when electricity enters in. When God made man, God made man so that he would change amazingly when Jesus enters. When our hearts become one with the heart of Jesus, and when the word of Jesus enters our hearts, it is no longer us—Jesus works inside of us.

So, I said to Soohyun, "Soohyun, when Jesus was in this world, He healed many sick people. And at that time, this is what Jesus said, 'Do you believe it shall be done according to your faith?' Jesus said that when you have faith, that's when He will work. The doctor says that you will be bedridden because of the spinal infection, and you will die. However, in the books of the gospel—Matthew, Mark, Luke, and John—not once did Jesus see the sick, ignore them, and walk away. Jesus healed everyone, and Jesus wants to heal you, too.

"If the electricity is going to work, the electrical lines have to be connected. In the same way, if the heart of Jesus and your heart become connected, then the spinal infection will be nothing at all. Now I'm going to teach you how to connect your heart to the heart of Jesus. In the very last chapter and last verse of the book of Matthew, Jesus said, '...and, lo, I am with you always, even unto the end of the world.' Jesus does not lie. Jesus will always be with us until the end of the world. But for Jesus to work inside of us, our hearts and His heart must become the same.

"Soohyun, let me teach you what the heart of Jesus is. When Jesus saw people who were sick, not once did He ignore them. He always healed them, and Jesus wants to heal you, too. Then, when you have the heart, 'Jesus wants to heal me. Then He will help me,' you become one in heart with Him."

I Was Sick in My Own Eyes, but I Was Healed in the Eyes of the Lord

In 1987, I suffered terribly due to a stomach ulcer. My stomach ulcer began around March of that year. For three months, no matter what I ate, it gave me diarrhea. I was unable to eat properly. The hospital gave me some prescribed medicine, and it made me feel very good inside. I felt fine, but after one week, even the medication became useless. I could barely eat any food.

At that time, I needed to go to many conferences as the guest speaker. These conferences were scheduled months in advance, so I had to go. However, because the people who were hosting the conferences had no idea about the condition my stomach was in, the chances were good that they were preparing lots of greasy food to treat me as the guest speaker. And since I barely got to eat because of the ulcer, I lost 7 kg of weight during those three months. At that time my weight was 70 kilograms. When I lost 7 kilograms, my pants were loose, and my suit was loose.

One day, I woke up early from my sleep. Usually, during the summer, we have retreats and many events. With my body in the condition it was in, there was no way I was going to get through all the summer events. So, I prayed to God, "God, my stomach hurts so much. God, please heal my stomach. I'm not sure that I can get through the summer events with my body like this." And while praying, a Bible verse I knew came to mind. It was Mark chapter 11, verse 24, which read, *Therefore I say unto you, What things soever ye desire, when ye pray, believe that ye receive them, and ye shall have them.*

It is so easy how a disease gets healed. God promised that what things so ever you pray, if you believe it, you shall have it. According to these words, I prayed that my stomach would be healed since it hurt. It says that I should believe that I have received the answer, then I shall have the answer. It was so easy. It was to be done according to my faith. I believed that I was healed, but there was a problem. I needed to eat breakfast soon.

Even just having a little porridge would give me diarrhea, so I never even thought about eating kimchi. However, if I believe that I'm all healed, I should eat the kimchi. If I don't eat the kimchi, it means that I don't believe that my stomach is completely healed. This is difficult. Even though I'm a pastor, I saw that I had no faith. And when I thought about eating the kimchi, I got very scared. The doctor said to me, "You need to be careful. Pastor, your stomach walls have become thin like wet sheets of paper. One small mistake, and your stomach could burst. And if your stomach bursts, you will die within 24 hours."

I had no confidence to eat kimchi because eating just porridge gave me diarrhea. I felt that eating kimchi would lead to a big disaster. However, the Bible clearly says, "What things soever ye desire, when ye pray, believe that ye receive them, and ye shall have them." That's exactly what it said. The word of the Bible is that it shall be done exactly so. I realized, "Ah, I'm not believing the words of the Bible right now. But if I believe now, it shall be done. My stomach is healed. Because if I believe according to the words of the Bible, it shall be done so. I believe that my stomach is completely healed, so my stomach is healed."

And so, I went to go have breakfast. That day, many guests came to my house, so my wife prepared a lot of food. But on one side of the table were a few sheets of seaweed, a small amount of meat, and a little bit of porridge. They were put there for me to eat. I pushed that food aside and picked up the big bowl of rice to eat. I also ate kimchi and bean paste soup.

My wife saw me doing this and she was shocked. "Honey, what do you think you're doing?" she asked. I told her, "Don't worry, I'm all healed." When I tell my wife she has no faith, there's nothing she can say about that. She was afraid that I might say that she doesn't have faith if she continued to worry. So, she just walked away without saying another word.

Usually, I eat very fast. Before getting married, I needed to read the Bible more. So, I trained myself to cut down on the time I used on other things. Of course, I cut down on my sleeping time, but I also cut down on the time I did everything else. I never shower for more than five minutes, and I never took more than two minutes to eat a meal. I would conserve my time in order to read the Bible. Living like that became a habit. So, I eat food very fast.

Occasionally, these days, as I dine with special guests, sometimes they're not even halfway finished, but I have already eaten everything. I would have to continue to eat more side dishes at times. That day, I ate all my food, and the other guests were not even halfway done. And as soon as I put my spoon down, my stomach began to hurt. It was unbearable. I told my guests, "Please excuse me." Then I got up from the table and headed straight for the restroom.

I was having a very bad bout of diarrhea, and it was very painful. I thought to myself, "What if this continues and I die? No, wait. I'm completely healed." But then there was a voice I heard from within, that said, "If you are healed, you should not be hurting. Your stomach hurts and you have diarrhea. Is that healed?" As I listened to that voice, I began to think, "Well, maybe I'm not healed."

Then suddenly a certain thought came to mind. "When Jesus went to Jairus' house, who was a ruler of the synagogue, Jairus' daughter was dead. But Jesus told everyone that she was sleeping. Everyone laughed when they heard that. They said, 'You can't even tell the difference between being dead and sleeping? If she's sleeping, she should be breathing. Her body should be warm. But this child's body is cold and she's not even breathing. But you're saying she's sleeping? She's dead.'" In people's eyes, she was surely dead. But Jesus said that she was sleeping. The child came back to life according to the words of Jesus. Even though I'm sick in my own eyes, my stomach is all healed in the eyes of the Lord.

And so, for lunch, I finished a whole bowl of rice. But then, I had diarrhea again. In the evening, I was invited to a dinner, so I went. I don't like to eat out unless it's a very special occasion. That day I was invited to a buffet at the Hyatt Hotel, so I had to go. As I went into the restaurant, I thought to myself, "Since my stomach hurts, I'm just going to have a little bit of porridge and that'll be it." But then I thought to myself, "No, I'm all healed." I ate a lot of food. My stomach was popping out on the way home. When I woke up the next morning, I could feel that my stomach had been completely healed, exactly 24 hours after I prayed and believed. My stomach was completely healed.

From then on, my stomach became very healthy and

strong. Before that, I was unable to eat any kind of flour-based foods or anything sour, but I can eat anything very well now. The Word of God is very accurate. When we read the words of the Bible, and add in man's thoughts, that's when it becomes a problem. I told Soohyun about this. In my eyes I have a disease, but if you pray and believe that you are healed, then the heart of Jesus and your heart become one.

Jesus says that you are healed. Jesus says that you are clean. If you really believe that Jesus has healed you, He will live and work inside you—it comes to pass exactly as promised. Right then, I saw the look in Soohyun's eyes begin to change. I put my hands on Soohyun's head and prayed for her. Then, I returned to Seoul. About four months later, Soohyun sent me a letter. It was a letter written on a yellow flowery paper with small, neat handwriting. The letter read: "Dear Pastor Ock Soo Park: How are you? I am Soohyun Choi, from Gumi. Do you remember me?" She mentioned in her letter that she started walking. She said that although she was not very good at the moment, she was going to show me that she is walking, very soon.

After one month, Soohyun and her parents came to visit me in Seoul. Her body had become very healthy. I was so happy to see her. I took her by the hand, and we walked around my office once. Her steps were slow, but I was so thankful that she was walking. During the International Youth Fellowship World Camp, which opened up a few months later, Soohyun participated and even competed in the short distance marathon. She ended up finishing 300th place out of 800 students.

The doctor told Soohyun that she was going to die soon, but I told her, "No, you will live. Your disease will be healed. God never lies. However, there is one condition. All you have to do is believe that Jesus will surely heal your disease. If you believe, then the disease is not your problem, but Jesus' problem."

After that, I forgot about Soohyun, but four months later, Soohyun sent me a letter, and came to my office to visit me with her parents. I heard that Soohyun even has a job. God truly is alive and working in our midst. However, the problem is that people simultaneously believe and doubt. "It looks like it's going to work," or "It looks like it's not going to work." Most people remain at this crossroads. If people have the faith that it will be done, that's when God works inside of us. Whenever people have a sickness or various problems, God will live and work if they have precise faith.

Covered with the Smoke and Sprinkled with the Blood

Today we're going to be talking about Leviticus chapter 16, verse 11. *And Aaron shall bring the bullock of the sin offering, which is for himself, and shall make an atonement for himself, and for his house, and shall kill the bullock of the sin offering which is for himself.*

What does the Bible say about what happens after this is finished? Leviticus chapter 6, verse 12 reads, *And he shall take a censer full of burning coals of fire from off the altar before the Lord, and his hands full of sweet incense beaten small, and bring it within the vail.* The mercy seat was to be covered by the smoke from the incense altar. God was saying, "Put the tablets of stone, which have the commandments recorded on them, inside of the ark, close the lid, and cover the mercy seat with the smoke from the incense altar."

Then verse 14, says, *And he shall take of the blood of the bullock, and sprinkle it with his finger upon the mercy seat eastward; and before the mercy seat shall he sprinkle of the blood with his finger seven times.* This means before coming to the ark, there is blood sprinkled there already. And then verse 15 says, *Then shall he kill the goat of the sin offering, that is for the people, and bring his blood within the vail, and do with that blood as he did with the blood of the bullock, and sprinkle it upon the mercy seat, and before the mercy seat.* In order to preach about this effectively, I think I should make an ark, put the Ten Commandments inside, close the lid, and show you the angels covering the lid with their wings. Then, I think you'd get a better feel for it. But none of that is prepared this time, so please listen carefully instead.

The blood was sprinkled on the mercy seat. Why is that? Suppose, for example, a person committed a sin, and it is the law that judges that sin. That is why you pull out the Ten Commandments and point out, "You committed theft. You lied, so, you need to receive destruction." When a person commits sins, the law must be manifested. However, blood was now sprinkled everywhere. This means that even though they have committed sins, the law should not be brought out because Jesus has already shed His blood to pay the price for sins. The sins have already been washed. Therefore, this is telling us to not bring out the law.

All of this is testifying that the blood of Jesus has forgiven our sins. They are afraid that people might not know this. So, the blood is put on the eastern side of the mercy seat. You come from the east, and before you face the mercy seat, there is blood already sprinkled there. Then, more blood is applied to the top of the mercy seat. What God wants the most is for the ark to be not open. The Word of God tells us to not look at the law again. "I should not commit adultery. I should not murder. I should not sin." People try to live this way, but it doesn't work.

The law condemns us. It does not give us the strength to refrain from sin. The Holy Spirit gives us the power to defeat sin when it enters us. There is no power to overcome sin within the law. There is no mercy in the law, only curses. If you commit sin and come before the law, you have to be cursed. That's why God does not want to establish a relationship with us under the law.

The Life of Being Led by the Holy Spirit, Being Free from the Law of Sin and Death

God tells us to stop looking to the law. He is saying, "That law, it will not do." Romans chapter 8 speaks on this. *There is therefore now no condemnation to them which are in Christ Jesus, who walk not after the flesh, but after the Spirit. For the law of the Spirit of life in*

Christ Jesus hath made me free from the law of sin and death. (Romans 8:1-2)

God does not want us to be tied down to the law. Just because people are tied down to the law it does not mean they do not break it. With the law of the spirit, the heart of wanting to commit sin disappears from us if the heart of Jesus enters ours. We get to live bright and blessed lives. We can have the faith that Jesus will heal my disease. The law was given to us to help us realize what sin is. So, it is pointless for us to try to keep the law well after realizing sin. So, what should we do after realizing sin? Accept the words of the Bible by faith—that's when the heart of Jesus enters ours and begins to lead us.

I will put my laws into their hearts, and in their minds I will write them. (Hebrews 10:16) Here, in Hebrews chapter 10, verse 16, God is telling us to no longer have a relationship with Him based on the law. God is telling us to not argue about this and that over the law. He is telling us to believe that we have been made holy through the blood of Jesus Christ, which has washed away all our sins. It's nonsense to try and be humble, saying, "Oh, I am a sinner." To be truly humble is to throw away your thoughts and believe in the Word of God. God washed our sins away through the blood of Jesus. He had the law of the spirit of life lead us, which has nothing to do with the law.

There is therefore now no condemnation to them which are in Christ Jesus, who walk not after the flesh, but after the Spirit. For the law of the Spirit of life in Christ Jesus hath made me free from the law of sin and death. (Romans

8:1-2) If we say we are free from the law (the law of sin and death), there are some people who will question if that means you can sin as much as you want. This is because that person is under the law.

People commit lots of sins. However, if they enter into the law of the spirit of life, they become distant from sin since the heart of Jesus watches over our hearts. Because we are led by the Holy Spirit of God our eyes to see the Bible change. And, our lives change, too, since we realize and experience the heart of Jesus.

What God hates the most is for us to be tied down to the law. What kind of people need a law? People who do not have the law of the spirit need the law. People who have received the forgiveness of sins have the Holy Spirit of life inside of them. The law of the Holy Spirit leads our lives to be bright, holy, and humble. It is so amazing how this works. There is no condemnation without the law. As we become free from sin and are led by the Holy Spirit, we live bright and blessed lives.

Unfortunately, many people are tied down to the law today. They think things like, "I was unable to keep the Sabbath Day. I lied." Becoming perfect does not free us from that—it's about accepting the Word of God by faith, which also happens to be the heart of Jesus Christ. If the heart of Jesus enters your heart, then your life changes. Your eyes to read the Bible also completely change.

Even after receiving salvation, even though I am nothing at all, I saw God living and working inside of me many times. When my stomach was sick, Jesus healed me completely. Even when I was in danger because my heart was very sick, He healed me completely, so that I could live with a healthy body. It was so amazing and thankful that God was leading me to live with a healthy body. Let us walk together with God. And let us walk with Jesus. Jesus has made us holy. God is telling us to no longer look at the law. God is telling us to close the law up, and do not open the lid. Do not look at the law but abide in the law of the spirit of life.

Even though I am a nobody, I saw God working continuously after getting saved. After being saved, I had a lot of big hardships. There were people who went against me. There were even people who accused me of running a cult and attacked me without any basis. There were people who claimed that we don't pray. They said things that were made up in their own minds, which is completely different from the truth. These are people who knew nothing about us, but it's not a problem because God is continuously opening doors for us. He opened the doors to the whole world. The leaders of Christianity in the world are joining us. I cannot express how thankful I am.

We believe in Jesus. Is the Lord holy? Then, we, too, are holy. Is the Lord righteous? Then, we, too, are righteous. We were not holy. We were dirty and evil. However, the blood of Jesus made us righteous. People under the law, they say, "You have committed sins. Then you shall be judged according to the law." However, the Bible says this, "I will forgive their iniquities, and I will remember their sins no more." In Jeremiah chapter 31, verse 34, it reads, ...*for I will forgive their iniquity, and I will remember their sin no more.* This is the new covenant.

A long time ago, we needed to refrain from sin and do good. But the new covenant is all about accepting what God has done. We aren't the ones who forgive our sins— it is God who forgives our sins. We don't do something to receive the forgiveness of sins. God has already forgiven our sins. God sent Jesus to this world, and He has carried all of our sins away. Jesus washed all of our sins away through His blood that was shed on the cross. Jesus' blood was sprinkled on the mercy seat, which was on top of the ark. Where did God say He wanted to meet us? He wanted to meet us at the mercy seat, and with the lid of the ark completely closed.

The words of Leviticus that we read today clearly tells us the fact that the closed lid of the ark was to never be opened. They had to even cover the top of the ark with the smoke from the incense altar. The angels covered the mercy seat, and blood was sprinkled on top of everything. God said, "I no longer want to be with you through the law. There is a new law. The law of the spirit of life." It's the heart of Jesus Christ. If the heart of Jesus enters ours, then we become thankful. We get to live for the gospel of God. There is no law that says we have to do these things, but when the heart of Jesus enters our hearts, we get to preach the word every day.

When I read the Bible, it is so amazing. So, I read it every day, and also preach the Word of God every day. I started our missionary school in 1976, and I preached the word to the theology students. I preached the word at conferences. I would lead the service and preach the word. I preached the word so many times. There were many pastors who heard those words and became born again. I sincerely wish that all of them become precious servants of God who will lead many people to be free from sin.

Now we are beginning a new theology school in America. We have started with recruiting pastors and born-again Christians, talking about how the blood of Jesus Christ washed away their sins, how to live by faith, and how the Holy Spirit resides and works inside of us. We also want to teach how to walk with the Holy Spirit. Once they learn just a few principles of spiritual life, spiritual life becomes easy because it is not something you do—it is something that God does.

The First Woman Who Is Judged by the Law of the Spirit of Life

After I had that big dinner at the Hyatt Hotel, I fell asleep and woke up the next morning. My stomach was completely healed. All I did was believe in the Word of God, and I believed the promise of God. Now everyone, be free from your own thoughts. If you accept the words of Jesus, your heart will be like the heart of Jesus. Then, the heart of Jesus will work inside of you, and you will be able to believe in the Bible in a completely new way. In order to live that way, do not become tied down under the law again.

For the law of the Spirit of life in Christ Jesus hath

made me free from the law of sin and death. (Romans 8:2) Even without the law, the law of the Holy Spirit in our hearts makes us hate sin and leads us far away from evil. Before, we wanted to steal and have a lustful heart,. But, since the law told us not to do it, we tell ourselves, "I shouldn't commit adultery. I shouldn't steal." Now, the heart of Jesus is inside of us and it gives us the heart that hates those things. This is the love of Jesus Christ, which overflows in us.

The woman caught in the act of adultery was the first woman to be judged by the law of the Spirit of life. According to the law, she was supposed to be stoned to death, but Jesus told this woman, "Neither do I condemn thee." This woman was able to go back home with a deeply thankful heart. She realized, "I was supposed to be stoned to death, but Jesus saved me." In order to do that, Jesus wrote on the ground for her because God wrote the first law with His finger, too. The new covenant was written on the ground by Jesus with His finger.

The new covenant was basically saying, "I will forgive their iniquities and remember their sins no more." According to the promise of God, Jesus died for the woman's sins, and this woman's sins were washed clean. When this woman came back home, there was no way for her to push out her thankful heart. "I was led by a lustful heart, and I committed adultery. I was supposed to be stoned to death, but Jesus died instead of me. I should have been stoned, my head should have been broken open, my back should have been broken, my face should have been scarred, and I should have been bleeding. However,

Jesus loved me and saved me." When our hearts become filled with Jesus' heart, there is no room for a lustful heart. When our heart is full of thankfulness, there is no room for the hateful heart. There is also no room for ambition to enter. I cannot express in words how thankful this is. It is not about us having the heart, "I shouldn't commit adultery. I shouldn't steal. I shouldn't lie." Jesus enters our hearts, and He gives us peace and joy. Then all the problems that arise in us become Jesus' problems.

Be People Who Throw Away Their Own Thoughts and Believe the Word

My hair is gray, and now I am old. I was born again in 1962. In October of 2022, it will have been 60 years. I am thankful whenever I look over the days that have passed. I was a dirty sinner, but He cleansed me. During the last 60 years, God has done so many great and unspeakable things through a person like me. He stirred up the heart in me and led me to do all those works. I read the Bible and became born again. It was so precious and amazing.

In the beginning, I barely ever let the Bible out of my hands. I would only put the Bible down briefly when I washed my face. Otherwise, a Bible has always been in my hands, even when I slept at night. I have slept, holding the Bible. I am so thankful. It feels like yesterday that I was doing those things, but it has already been 60 years that have passed. I used to only commit sins and do evil deeds. But through Jesus, I have preached the gospel, and many people have changed and been used for this holy work. I am infinitely thankful about this.

I don't know how many more years I will live. However, by the guidance of the Lord, I want to preach all over the world about the fact that our sins have been clearly washed away through the blood Jesus shed on the cross. May we all throw our thoughts away and believe the word. If the word settles in your heart, then the Holy Spirit will lead you. Your life will become bright and happy.

Before I was born again, I was surrounded by nothing but darkness and despair. But from the day I got saved, God led my life so amazingly. I hope this will happen to you, too. May we all have the heart of Jesus Christ and become small Jesuses who shine brightly in this world. May we all work together and help the pastors around the world. We want to preach this gospel all over the world, and I believe God will give us the strength to do so, and that He will help us.

God is saying, "Do not open up the ark again."

But we are answering, "But we have committed sin. We need to be judged by the law."

If we refute God like that, this is what He will say, "That's why the blood of Jesus was shed. So, cut out the nonsense. Do not bring out the law again but abide under the law of the Spirit by grace." Within the precious Word of God, without any discomfort in front of God, I hope that you will be people who live happily and gloriously and then come before God in heaven.

Chapter 5

en the Blood of
ssover Lamb Is
Placed in Your Heart

When the Blood of the Passover Lamb Is Placed in Your Heart

The Bible is the living Word of God. It doesn't matter who you are—you are no longer your former self when the words of the Bible enter and settle in your heart. A new strength arises when the word enters and leads you, and you become filled with thankfulness—your heart begins to have peace and happiness. Let us read from Exodus chapter 12, verses 1-14.

And the Lord spake unto Moses and Aaron in the land of Egypt saying, this month shall be unto you the beginning of months: it shall be the first month of the year to you. Speak ye unto all the congregation of Israel, saying, In the tenth day of this month they shall take to them every man a lamb, according to the house of their fathers, a lamb for an house: And if the household be too little for the lamb, let him and his neighbour next unto his house take it according to the number of the souls; every man according to his eating shall make your count for the lamb. Your lamb shall be without blemish, a male of the first year: ye shall take it out from the sheep, or from the goats: And ye shall keep it up until the fourteenth day of the same month: and the whole assembly of the congregation of Israel shall kill it in the evening. And they shall take of the blood, and strike it on the two side posts and on the upper door post of the houses, wherein they shall eat it. And they shall eat the flesh in that night, roast with fire, and unleavened bread; and with bitter herbs they shall eat it. Eat not of it raw, nor sodden at all with water, but roast with fire; his head with his legs, and with the purtenance thereof. And ye shall let nothing of it remain until the morning; and that which remaineth of it until the morning ye shall burn with fire. And thus shall ye eat it; with your loins girded, your shoes on your feet, and your staff in your hand; and ye shall eat it in haste: it is the Lord's passover. For I will pass through the land of Egypt this night, and will smite all the firstborn in the land of Egypt, both man and beast; and against all the gods of Egypt I will execute judgment: I am the Lord. And the blood shall be to you for a token upon the houses where ye are: and when I see the blood, I will pass over you, and the plague shall not be upon you to destroy you, when I smite

the land of Egypt. And this day shall be unto you for
a memorial; and ye shall keep it a feast to the Lord
throughout your generations; ye shall keep it a feast
by an ordinance for ever. (Exodus 12:1-14)

The many stories in the Bible contain things that God wants to teach us. The most important factor is how to believe in Jesus in order to be freed from sin and become the people of God. There are many things the Bible speaks about in this regard.

In the past, I attended church, but was always living in doubt. I would ask myself, "Have I really received the forgiveness of sins? I have prayed a lot for my sins to be forgiven, but have they truly been forgiven? If I die now, would I be able to go to heaven?" That was how I lived before, and the day the Word of God entered my heart, I started to change. I started to believe the word, and the word resided in me and worked in me. I witnessed the power of God appear through me, and it was not of myself.

As a New World of the Heart Was Formed Inside of the Maidservant

In 2 Kings chapter 5, of the Old Testament, there is the leper named Captain Naaman. He was a captain of Syria. One day, while at war against Israel, he captured a young girl in the battlefield and brought her home. This girl became the maidservant to Naaman's wife. It must have been so hard to be a maidservant. She must have thought to herself, "I believe in God, but why did God allow me to be captured and taken captive? When will I ever get to go home?" She had a lot of sadness and suffering. She wanted to return to her hometown. She missed her parents and siblings, and she wanted to see her friends. On top of all that, she became worried after discovering Captain Naaman had leprosy, "What if I also get leprosy?"

She lived that way for a while, but then a new world formed in her heart: "The captain is a leper. If he meets the Prophet Elisha in Samaria, he will be healed quickly. This is the reason I was taken captive—to be the link for Captain Naaman to get healed of his leprosy. That is why God sent me here. I'd better tell the lady of the house about this. The captain would be so happy if he gets cured of his leprosy. This entire household will change. They'll be so happy, too. And after the captain gets saved, we're going to have Bible study every day."

Even though people are in the same situation, some live in a completely different world depending on what leads their hearts. Without knowing the will of God, if you just thought that you were taken captive, then you would think, "God did not protect me. What did I do wrong? When will I ever get to see my parents again? Do I have to live as a servant for the rest of my life? What if this continues, and I get leprosy?" In this state, ten out of ten, 100 out of 100, there is nothing but worries. However, a different heart entered the heart of the maidservant despite being in the same situation: "Ah, the captain is a leper. If he goes to the prophet in Samaria, he can be healed right away. God allowed me to be taken captive to teach them about this. The captain getting healed from his leprosy will improve the relations between Syria and Israel, and there will be no wars." Your life changes if your heart changes.

I, too, went through a lot of hardships when I was young. During the Korean War in 1951, my mother passed away. My older brother went into the army after that, and my father was in the battlefield providing support. Within a short period of time, my big brother and both my parents were no longer at home.

At that time, my eldest sister was only 15 years old. We didn't know what we were going to eat, or how we were going to live. One night, I heard a strange sound, and I opened my eyes. My oldest sister could not cry in front of us, so she cried all by herself while we were sleeping. The weather was cold, and there was nothing to eat. My oldest sister barely ever ate anything.

From a young age, I diligently attended church. I went to services, prayed, and read the Bible. However, my heart was always in darkness. I was always sad and in pain. I did not know how I was going to survive. Then in 1962, my life started to change as I discovered in the words of the Bible that my sins were forgiven—God worked inside of me.

Even now, I do not believe that I am the one doing the work I do. I was a person with so many problems. However, reading the Bible after being saved was very different than when I wasn't saved. My life completely changed as the words of the Bible entered my heart.

The maidservant, who was serving in the house of Captain Naaman, the leper, received a new heart and her life completely changed, too.

One day, the maidservant told Captain Naaman's wife, "Madam, there is something I need to tell you."

"What is it?"

"The captain has an illness."

"Yeah, so? What about it?"

"Well, what I mean to say, is that there is a prophet named Elisha from my country. He has healed many people of their diseases. If Captain Naaman goes to the prophet, he will surely be healed of his disease."

"Nonsense."

"Madam, think about it. If Captain Naaman goes to Samaria and returns without being healed of his leprosy, that would be so painful for me. I would live the rest of my life in suffering. Why would I tell you this? But I am absolutely sure that if he goes to the servant of God, he will surely be healed of his disease."

"Are you out of your mind? Does that make any sense?"

"It really is true, Madam. He will be healed of his disease. Please tell the captain about this."

That night, Naaman's wife told Naaman about what she heard from her maidservant. He replied, "Elisha? I've heard of him. I heard there is a prophet of God living in Samaria. And he works with the power of God."

"You've heard of him?"

"Yeah, it's true."

"The maidservant knows Elisha very well. She says that you will surely be healed if you go visit him."

"Really? Bring her here." She came and Captain Naaman asked her, "Hey, how can you be so sure of this?"

"Captain, I am very sure. Elisha is a man of God."

"Has he ever healed leprosy before?"

"He hasn't healed lepers before, but he has healed many other diseases. He's even raised someone from the dead."

"Wow, that's true. I've heard about that myself."

"Captain Naaman, you should go to Samaria. Once you meet the prophet, Elisha, your leprosy will be healed."

The President Who Received the Forgiveness of Sins and Held My Hand Tightly

I do work for the youth. The Paraguayan ambassador to Korea often attended our events, and he and I became close. One day, the ambassador came to me and said, "I consider you my big brother, Pastor Ock Soo Park. I wanted a Korean name that's similar with yours, so I named myself, Dae Soo Park." The ambassador is younger than me, and that's what he said.

Some time passed, and the ambassador came to me with a sincere request. "Pastor, there is something I'm worried about." I asked him what the matter was, and he replied, "The president of Paraguay will be visiting Korea. I have to oversee his 3-day itinerary while he's in Korea. The president of your home country visiting the country you're serving as an ambassador is a once-in-a-lifetime experience. If I serve the president well for those three days and he is satisfied, I could become a minister or even the prime minister. However, the embassy does not have a large budget. I am so worried and do not know what to do. I thought about it a lot, and I think it's a good idea to hold a concert for the president since he enjoys music. My favor I ask of you is to send the Gracias Choir to perform."

At that time, we were having a Bible Crusade at the Jamsil Arena, so the Gracias Choir was staying in Seoul. I told the choir director about the situation, and she selected a few members from the choir to put a concert together for the president of Paraguay.

At the Bible Crusade, I needed to stand at the pulpit to preach no later than 8:20 pm. So, I thought that it would be okay to attend the meeting with the president at the Paraguayan embassy until about 7:30 pm. So, I arrived at the embassy, just 30 minutes before the concert was scheduled to start. The ambassador knew I was there, so he called me, saying, "Pastor, come to the ninth floor." When I went to the ninth floor, the president was there, with his head secretary, two ministers, and the ambassador. I spoke with the president for about 30 minutes. At first, I did not know what to talk about because it was the first time I was able to meet the president of a country in my entire life. However, the ambassador, who was standing right next to me, helped me out. I was able to speak to the president about working for the youth. It became time for me to go to the Bible Crusade, so I gave him the book I wrote, *The Secret of the Forgiveness of Sin and Being Born Again,* as a gift.

Two days later, the ambassador called me and said, "Pastor, the president finished reading your book. He has sent you an invitation letter. It would be great to have you visit Paraguay." I wrote a letter back to the president,

which read: "Your Excellency, Mr. President: thank you
for your invitation. The World Camp hosted by IYF opens
in Paraguay in February. If it would be okay with you, I
would like to go then to meet with you."

I ended up traveling to Paraguay in February. It was
the first time in my life being invited by the president of
a country, so everything felt different. When the airplane
landed at the international airport in Paraguay, the
security personnel boarded the plane. They allowed all
the other passengers to remain seated, but they picked me
out and had me deplane. While waiting in the VIP room
of the airport, the officials who received me took care of
all the paperwork needed for my entry. My security detail
protected me 24 hours a day at the hotel room where I
stayed. And they escorted me whenever I went out.

Before meeting the president, I called the head
secretary and asked, "How much time do I get to meet
with the president?"

He replied, "40 minutes. It may go longer if the
president wants to speak more. However, if he does not
give us a sign, then, when your 40 minutes are up, you
must leave."

I answered him, "I understand."

I needed to talk to the president about the forgiveness
of sins and being born again during the 40-minute
meeting. Because the president likes music, I also took
two members of the Gracias Choir with me. However,
if they were to sing three songs, that would take
approximately 10 minutes. Then, if we subtracted another
5 minutes for greeting one another and saying hello, then

that would leave only 25 minutes remaining. Therefore, I needed to conserve the time. I told the choir members, "I have a lot of things to say to the president." In the end, I asked them to please not take up any of my 25 minutes. Then I prepared what I would say to the president for the 25 minutes, and I revised it again and again.

The next day, I arrived at the presidential palace. When the people who came with me finished saying their hellos to the president, it took exactly five minutes. And after the Gracias Choir members sang three songs; I immediately preached the word after they finished. I read the words that were written in Acts chapter 13, verse 22, *And when he had removed him, he raised up unto them David to be their king; to whom also he gave their testimony, and said, I have found David the son of Jesse, a man after mine own heart, which shall fulfil all my will.*

I then explained the verse to him, "Your Excellency, when you become one in heart with God, and you come to have the same will as God, God establishes you. I want to tell you what it means to become one in heart with God." I spoke to the president about receiving the forgiveness of sins through the blood of Jesus Christ. The president listened and received the forgiveness of sins. He was holding back tears, and his face turned red. He held my hand very tightly. I thought my hand was going to break. The president was so happy. As I witnessed this, I, too, was very happy. It was something I will never forget.

I was coming out of the president's office, and we were getting into the car to leave when the head secretary called me on my cell phone, saying, "The president will be in attendance, tonight, at the IYF World Camp." Ten minutes later, I received another phone call, which said, "The president has told all the ministers to attend the IYF World Camp tonight." That afternoon, it was sheer chaos at the camp venue. Many people from the president's security team came to confirm the event's security. That night, I sat shoulder to shoulder with the president.

Since then, I was able to meet with him and speak with him multiple times. The president also visited Korea three times. How is it that I can meet with the heads of states? I'm a person who preaches the gospel. When God wants the gospel to be preached to the heads of state, God makes the opportunities to meet with them. It was not easy, but if God does it, nothing is impossible.

Until now, I've met about 30 presidents, kings, and prime ministers, some, of whom, I've met five or six times. I preached the gospel each and every time I met them. Not all of them became born again, but most of them received the forgiveness of sins. In Muslim countries, whenever I preach the gospel, they do not accept the word very well. I'm a person who is quite distant from people like presidents. However, God is achieving these things through me, and I'm so thankful about that.

People Whose Lives Change When the Heart of Jesus Entered

How should we believe in order to believe well? How should we believe to become born again? How should we believe to receive the forgiveness of sins? How can you distinguish if a person truly is born again, or not? The Word of God shows us these things very clearly. People live with their own thoughts, experiences, and knowledge. And then Jesus enters their hearts. After Jesus enters their hearts, no one lives the same way they did before. Before Jesus, people lived according to their own thoughts. However, the people who have Jesus in their hearts were led by Him when they prophesied, when they prayed, and when their diseases were healed. Jesus then works inside of them with power. Their lives completely change because of that. I cannot express how thankful I truly am.

A long time ago, a lady who attended my church was very overweight. One time, she called me, and said, "Pastor,..." and she asked me to listen to her story. When I sat down and listened to her story, she told me that she could not sleep at night. She said she barely got 15 or 20 minutes of sleep a night. Her insomnia caused her to gain weight. When she weighed 60 kg, she thought to herself, "How did I gain so much weight?" However, she continued to put on more weight. She went to 70kg, to 80kg, to 90kg, and even to 100 kg. She told me that she continued to put on weight.

This lady had a very sad past. Because of that, she was unable to sleep. However, she said that after she received the forgiveness of sins, she got two full hours of sleep a night. Her life completely changed from that point on. The most joyous thing that happened to me after I became a pastor was that my father received the forgiveness of sins three days prior to passing away. For those three days, he became a completely transformed person—I was so thankful.

What a wonderful change in my life has been wrought, since Jesus came into my heart. And my sins which were many are all washed away, since Jesus came into my heart. I sang this hymn so many times in my life. Then there is another hymn that goes like this: *Oh, Happy day, oh, happy day, when Jesus washed my sins away.*

In the past, I sang these songs with my own lips. However, they were not sung from my heart. However, after Jesus came into my heart, I had no choice but be changed. I went to preach the gospel in a place called Apkokdong after receiving spiritual training in missionary school. There was a middle-aged lady who was older than I was at the time, who received the forgiveness of sins. That lady changed so much.

Some time afterward, a young man enrolled in the missionary school we were running. During his interview, he told me how he arrived at our missionary school. He was a soccer player and really loved the sport from a young age. His life's dream was to play on Korea's national team and compete in the FIFA World Cup. He daydreamed about kicking the ball into the back of the net. This young man was a soccer player in college, but one day after practice, he felt kind of sick. He asked himself, "Did I practice too hard?" and took a break. However, he did not get any better, rather, he grew worse and worse. He was examined at the hospital after his condition deteriorated—he was diagnosed with tuberculosis.

These days, people are cured of their tuberculosis with medication. However, in the 1970s, it was a very scary disease. Tuberculosis is very contagious. The tuberculosis bacterium that come out of the mouths of those infected would become airborne.

Because this young man could no longer stay at the dormitory for school athletes, he had to quit everything and return to his hometown. The members of his family who lived at his house in his hometown were his widowed mother, his older brother and his wife, and his nephews.

A few days after he went home, his older brother said to him, "Hey, come here for a minute."

He replied, "Yes, brother."

"I know I shouldn't be saying something like this to you in your condition. However, I need to say it. If it were only you and I living in this house, everything would be fine. But your young nephews are all living here. If you live with us, then all my children will also catch tuberculosis and die. So, I need you to leave this house."

After hearing that, he could see that everything his older brother said was right. So, he replied, "Yes, brother, I understand. It was very thoughtless of me to come here in the first place." He got up and left right away. Nobody tried to stop him from leaving. His mother was just standing to one side and crying; however, she did not try to stop him, either.

It was early winter, but this young man left home wearing just a set of thin clothes. It was very cold. He did not know where he was going to sleep, or how he was going to eat. He felt completely lost. By the time night fell, he still had not found a place to sleep. So, he went to this house that was right outside of the village. It was not really a house people lived in; it was used as the storage facility that housed coffin carriages. He thought to himself that if he slept there, he would at least be sheltered from the wind. It was kind of scary there. He hadn't eaten anything all day long and was very hungry. Then, he contemplated this and that, thinking, "Winter is coming. I will probably freeze to death like this." Then he fell asleep.

The following morning, he went to the creek to wash his face when somebody called out his name. "Heejin!" When he turned around, it was a lady from the village. She told him, "Hey, would you like to come with me?"

He asked her, "Where are we going?"

"I'm going to church."

He followed that lady to her church. However, they were having their service in a house. About ten people were gathered, and there was a middle-aged lady preaching the word from the Bible. She was the lady I mentioned before, who received salvation through me when I had preached the gospel in Apkokdong.

He sat there, leaning against the wall, and listening to her preaching. However, this young man had been shivering in the cold for such a long time, but now, he was in a warm room, so he began to feel very sleepy. He still has no idea how long he slept, but when he opened his eyes after someone woke him up, the service had already ended and most of the people had left. Only a few who remained, and they were preparing to eat lunch.

They woke him up and asked that he eat lunch with them.

He thought to himself, "I have tuberculosis, is it okay for me to eat with them? Should I tell them I have tuberculosis? What if I do, and they won't let me eat?" He hesitated for a minute, but then started to eat. He was so thankful. After having lunch, the lady who preached the sermon during service brought a Bible and spoke with him. He heard how the blood of Jesus washed away his sins. That day was the first time this young man went to a church, but he listened to the words of the Bible and received the forgiveness of sins. He was so thankful. They also offered him dinner, and he ate that, too.

He returned to the village after the evening service ended. The lady who brought him to church went home, and this young man went back to the coffin carriage storage facility. When he laid down and thought about what had happened that day, he was so thankful. He was thankful he got to eat two meals, and he was very thankful he had received the forgiveness of sins. He prayed for the first time in his life: "God, I don't know how to pray. The weather is cold, and I think I'm going to freeze to death. Please, give me a place to sleep."

The following day, one elder of the village came looking for him. He said, "Hey, Heejin, would you come over here?"

"Yes, how are you?"

"Hey, where were you yesterday?"

"I went to church yesterday."

"What? You believe in Jesus?"

"It was my first time yesterday."

"I was looking for you all day."

"Why?"

"I needed to tell you something."

This person was an owner of a large orchard by the mountains. This man worked very hard from the spring to the fall, and harvested apples from his orchard. After he sold them all, there was no need for him to stay at the orchard anymore. He would go home and spend the winter with his family. So, he needed someone to maintain the orchard while he was away. Then the man heard about this young person and asked him to live in his apple orchard. He said, "Hey, you can sleep there. It's a nice place. There are lots of branches I cut down, and if you burn them in the furnace, it'll make the room warm."

The young man went to the orchard, washed a rag, and cleaned the room. Then he started a fire in the furnace. The room got so warm. Then he thought to himself, "Did God just answer my prayer?" The day after he had prayed, he had immediately received a place where he could sleep.

While he stayed at the orchard, God also provided food for this young man to eat. Time passed, and it became spring. He went to a health clinic nearby and got himself examined. His tuberculosis was completely healed. He wanted to live for the gospel and entered our missionary school. Now, he is a very precious pastor, doing amazing work.

When we meet Jesus and receive the forgiveness of sins, we become one with Him. From then on, Jesus watches over our lives. Everybody is different from one another, but everyone changes after getting born again. People become joyful, happy, and delightful.

There are some people who are not born again, but speak as if they were. However, you can immediately tell. People, who are not born again, do not know this. On the other hand, the people who are born again can see this. The people who have Jesus in their hearts cannot be the same as those who do not. Those led by Jesus and those who live according to their own thoughts, are very different, whether they say a single word, walk one path, or read the Bible.

A long time ago in the past, when I used to read the Bible, I was unable to understand the meaning held within the Bible. However, when I read the Bible after being born again, I could see the heart of God with it. *What a wonderful change in my life has been wrought, since Jesus came into my heart.*

This change cannot be measured in terms of money, and no matter how much money you pay, this is something you cannot buy.

Passover, the Point for a New Beginning

We read about the Passover in Exodus chapter 12; we can see that the Israelites lived in Egypt for 430 years. God called Moses to lead them out, but the Pharaoh of Egypt did not want to let the Israelites go. He genuinely liked having them and putting them to work as slaves. However, God worked. He sent Egypt ten plagues. The last plague was to kill all the first born in Egypt. There was only one way to survive this. Exodus chapter 12 writes about that. *And the Lord spake unto Moses and Aaron in the land of Egypt saying, This month shall be unto you the beginning of months: it shall be the first month of the year to you. (Exodus 12:1-2)*

These words are about receiving the forgiveness of sins and being born again. Saying "let this month be the beginning of months" means that everything that came before was not valid. Whether it was March, May, or June in the past, but now, this month has officially become the beginning. No matter what you did in your life before you were born again, it's all nothing. Your new life begins from the day you are born again. No matter how much I read the Bible, I was unable to see any of this before I was born again. However, the Bible appeared completely new after I was born again.

In 2017, we started Christian Leaders Fellowship (CLF) and 750 pastors attended our first conference. For one week, I spoke to them about the forgiveness of sins. One pastor asked a pastor from our mission to come to his church. After his church members had gathered, he said, "Everyone, even though I am a pastor, I was not freed from sin until now. So, I was never able to preach about the gospel of the forgiveness of sins. But this time through attending the CLF, I became freed from sin. Now I, too, can talk about receiving the forgiveness of sins. However, I have invited one of the pastors here because the pastors of the Good News Mission know much more about this than I do. Let's first listen to the Word of God from him, and I will preach after that." Living without

Jesus is all in vain, and God does not reside within human calculations. However, the new year begins after you become born again.

The Judgement Passes Over You When the Blood Is Applied

The most important aspect to the rules of the Passover is the lamb. *Speak ye unto all the congregation of Israel, saying, In the tenth day of this month they shall take to them every man a lamb, according to the house of their fathers, a lamb for an house: (Exodus 12:3)*

And ye shall keep it up until the fourteenth day of the same month: and the whole assembly of the congregation of Israel shall kill it in the evening. And they shall take of the blood, and strike it on the two side posts and on the upper door post of the houses, wherein they shall eat it. (Exodus 12:6-7)

The Bible tells us that you had to kill the lamb and put its blood on both sides and the top of door.

For I will pass through the land of Egypt this night, and will smite all the firstborn in the land of Egypt, both man and beast; and against all the gods of Egypt I will execute judgment: I am the Lord. And the blood shall be to you for a token upon the houses where ye are: and when I see the blood, I will pass over you, and the plague shall not be upon you to destroy you, when I smite the land of Egypt. (Exodus 12:12-13)

On the night of the Passover, an angel went to every house and killed all the firstborn. However, it did not enter into the houses where the blood was put on the side and upper doorposts. Instead, the judgement would pass over the person. That is why it is called the Passover. If the blood of the lamb is put on the upper doorpost and side doorposts, the angel would just pass over that house to the next one. However, if there were no blood on any of the door posts, then the firstborn of that house would die.

I'd like to ask you, was this information a secret or not? It was a secret because only the Jews knew about this. The other people did not know about it at all. It was a secret from the Egyptians. If there were a Jewish person, who was close to any Egyptians, they most likely would have shared this information with them. If they know this precisely, then their firstborn will not die. However, if they do not know about this, then they will die.

The gospel is not a secret to those who have accepted the gospel, but it is to those who have not. Even though it's the same Bible, there are some people's eyes that see the way to escape the judgment. However, other people are unable to see it with their eyes. The people who cannot see this must receive destruction. If their eyes are opened and they see it, that person can live. This is the gospel.

Do Other Churches Say That They Are Sinners?

At the Passover, the people of Israel killed the lamb and put its blood on the side and upper doorposts. The side posts are the posts that stand upright on the sides of the door. The upper post is the horizontal piece of wood that connects the two side pillars of the door. That's where they apply the blood of the lamb. As the angel passes by that house and checks to see if there is blood on the door, if it sees blood, it will pass it over. The angel says, "Ah, the judgment has already come upon this house," and he will pass over the house. This was a secret known only to the people of Israel. The Egyptian people did not know this.

The people who go to church all say that Jesus died on the cross. They all say that He forgave their sins. However, the people who say this are divided into two groups. There are those who say, "Jesus died for me, but I'm a sinner," and those who say, "Jesus died for my sins, therefore, I'm righteous." If Jesus died for my sins, but I'm still a sinner, Jesus failed in dying for my sins. People who are not born again say, "Jesus died for my sins but I'm a sinner." They sing hymns that say, "I'm redeemed by the blood of the lamb," but when they pray, they say, "Lord, please forgive this sinner." They sing, "Oh, happy day! Oh, happy day, when Jesus washed my sins away," but then they pray, "Oh, Lord, please forgive this sinner."

Once, I was leading a seminar in Daegu. A reporter for the Daegu Daily Newspaper asked me for an interview. He asked, "Pastor, could you make some time for me please?"

I replied, "Sure."

Then the reporter asked me, "Pastor, I think that your sermons are different from other pastors' sermons. How is your church different from other churches?"

"Well, there's no short answer to that."

"Then, what is the biggest difference?"

"Do you attend church?"

"I've never been to church."

"But have you ever heard that Jesus died on the cross for our sins?"

"Well yes I've heard about that."

"Why was Jesus crucified?"

"Didn't He die for our sins?"

"Yes, that is the correct answer. The people of other churches say that Jesus was crucified for their sins, but since they commit sins, they say they are still sinners. There are many churches like that. However, our church says otherwise. Even though I have committed many sins because Jesus died on the cross for all of them, none of my sins remain. They have all been washed clean, and we say we have no sins. It may sound a little bit much, or a little bit proud, but it is definitely true that our sins have all been forgiven. They have been washed clean."

The reporter then asked me, "Do people at other churches say they're sinners?"

"Why don't you go and ask them?"

"Do they really say that? Even though Jesus was crucified for our sins? If they say that they are sinners, then what do they believe?"

This reporter had never once been to church. He's a person who only heard that Jesus died for people's sins. But even he understood that if Jesus died for our sins, our sins should be washed. The next day, an article ran in the Daegu Daily Newspaper about me. It filled the entire

Religion Section. The article was very well written.

Later on, that reporter called me on the phone. He told me that so many pastors of different churches called to complain after reading his article, that he was unable to keep up with his work. To the pastors who complained, he merely said, "I did not write my opinions. I interviewed Pastor Ock Soo Park and wrote down exactly what he said. A reporter is obligated to do so." The pastors were complaining and trying to argue, saying, "We're sinners. How could we be righteous?"

Your Excellency, How Did You Know That You Are a Sinner?

When I met the president of Ghana, he also said that he was a sinner.

So I asked him, "Your Excellency, how did you know that you're a sinner?"

He answered, "I've committed sins, so I'm a sinner, aren't I?"

So, I answered him, "Your Excellency, that is not true."

I opened up the Bible and read Romans chapter 3, verses 23 and 24. In verse 23, it says, *For all have sinned, and come short of the glory of God.* In verse 23, it states that surely everyone is a sinner. We have all sinned, and because of that, have come short of the glory of God. However, in verse 24, it says something to the contrary. *Being justified freely by his grace through the redemption that is in Christ Jesus.* In verse 24, there is Jesus. Jesus saved us. That's why God says that we are righteous.

We are not the judge. God is. And, God said that we are justified. I have committed many sins, and I told many lies and stolen many times. I committed so many sins, I cannot count them all. However, God sees me and says that I am righteous. He says that I have been justified. If God, the judge, says I'm righteous, then I'm righteous, am I not? If God says that I'm holy, then I'm holy, aren't I?

Who was delivered for our offences and was raised again for our justification. (Romans 4:25) On my own, I don't presume to know whether I'm a sinner or I am righteous—I simply believe the Word of God. No matter what anybody else says, if God says I'm justified, then, that's the correct answer. I am righteous. Even though I have lied, stolen, committed many sins, and have done lots of evil things, if God says I'm justified, I am justified. If God says that I'm righteous, I am righteous.

A person who believes in this manner is a person who believes in God. People tend to not believe the Bible but believe in their own thoughts. They consider themselves smarter than God. They believe in their own thoughts, and thus, call themselves sinners. However, God is our judge. In addition to that, God clearly says that we are righteous in the Bible.

If God Says That We Are Righteous, Then We Are Righteous, Are We Not?

Once, I went to the Dominican Republic. There were many pastors that had gathered. I got on the podium and said, "I am justified. I am righteous."

Right then, all of the pastors said that they had questions. I told them to go ahead and ask their questions, and they said, "Pastor, you never lied? Pastor, you never stole?"

I replied, "I've lied many times. So many times, in fact, that I've lost count. I've also stolen countless number of times."

"Then you're a sinner. How could you be righteous?"

I answered them, "I don't know. But what I do know is that God said that I am justified. That means that I am righteous, am I not? I refuse to believe in my thoughts. I believe in the Word of God. I committed many sins. Because I was hungry, I would break off wheat from other people's farms and I ate them. When the wheat would ripen, I would break off the wheat with my friends, and then we would take them into the mountains. We would go to the mountains, start a fire, roast the wheat, and rub them in our hands. Then we would blow on them and the shells would scatter. Then, we would eat the grains that remained. It was so tasty. We'd steal apples from other people's farms, and we stole so much. However, God said I'm righteous. People who believe their own thoughts say that they're sinners. But the people who believe the Word of God say that they are righteous. God says that I am righteous, and God says that He remembers my sins no more."

When I told the pastors in the Dominican Republic, "If God says I'm justified, then I'm righteous, am I not?" I went on to preach the word about that. Many pastors began to rush towards me after I finished preaching. I didn't know why. One of them asked to take a picture with me. Another asked me to sign his book. Another called me his father. It was because they listened to the Word of God and became righteous. I did not judge whether I was a sinner or righteous for myself. God judged me. In Romans chapter 3, verse 23, it describes us as sinners. But in verse 24, God says that we are justified. God, who is the true judge, said that we're righteous. Then, that is the correct answer. We are righteous. The amazing thing is that many people know about Romans chapter 3, verse 23. However, even though verse 24 is right next to verse 23, they don't know this verse. They are described as sinners in verse 23, but in verse 24, we have been justified through Jesus dying for us. If we're sinners even though Jesus didn't die, and we are sinners even though Jesus did die, then what was the point of Jesus dying?

In the Bible, there are so many words that say we are justified. Let's look at 1 Corinthians chapter 6, verse 10: *Nor thieves, nor covetous, nor drunkards, nor revilers, nor extortioners, shall inherit the kingdom of God.* Now, let's look at verse 11, which says, "And such were some of you…" This means that we have committed these kinds of sins. But what does it say after that?

And such were some of you: but ye are washed, but ye are sanctified, but ye are justified in the name of the Lord Jesus, and by the Spirit of our God. (1 Corinthians 6:11) It says that, "…but ye are washed, but ye are sanctified, but ye are justified…" These are not words from a judge or a president—they are written this way in the Word of

God. If God says we're washed, we're washed. If God says we're sanctified, we're sanctified. If God says we're justified, we're justified. Do not add your own thoughts to this. Are you more right than the Word of God? You're not. And, no matter how much you claim that you aren't, if God says you're righteous, then you're righteous.

God is the righteous judge, and God cannot call a sinner righteous. Does God call us justified when we are sinners? Not at all. We were sinners, but Jesus was crucified and washed away all of our sins. So, we are righteous in the eyes of God. If we had sins, God could never say we are justified. Through Jesus shedding His blood and dying, our sins have been washed, and we've been made righteous. We are righteous in God's eyes. That's why God says that we are justified.

When we look at ourselves through our own eyes, we appear to be sinners. However, God said that we are righteous. We should not believe our own thoughts but believe the Word of God. Even though it's very easy, and despite the fact that they go to church, many people say that they are sinners. This is the same thing as saying our sins have not been washed clean even though Jesus was crucified. Then, why would you want to believe in a Jesus who was crucified and was unable to wash away your sins? However, none of that is true. Jesus was crucified and forgave all of our sins forever.

But Christ being come an high priest of good things to come, by a greater and more perfect tabernacle, not made with hands, that is to say, not of this building; Neither by the blood of goats and calves, but by his own blood he entered in once into the holy place, having obtained eternal redemption for us. (Hebrews 9:11-12) Here, it says that Jesus obtained eternal redemption. That is how He made us holy. I was a sinner, but the blood of Jesus washed me as white as snow.

> *Oh I know I'm alive in the Lord and I strive,*
> *unto blood with the sin that would damn.*
> *As I walk in the light there is strength for the fight,*
> *I'm redeemed by the blood of the lamb.*

It doesn't make sense that even though people sing hymns like this, they say that they are sinners when they pray. I think it makes God dizzy. They say that they are redeemed, and then they say that they are sinners. It makes absolutely no sense. However, even though people do this, they have no idea what is wrong with it. I believe the Word of God. My judgment is not important. I committed sins, and I was a sinner. But Jesus washed those sins whiter than snow. God says I'm justified. Everyone, don't believe your thoughts. Believe the Word of God. The Bible says our sins have all been washed away.

And such were some of you: but ye are washed, but ye are sanctified, but ye are justified in the name of the Lord Jesus, and by the Spirit of our God. (1 Corinthians 6:11) Is there still anyone who says they are a sinner? Do not believe your thoughts. You are sinners when you look at yourselves from within your thoughts. This is because you have committed many sins. However, God says that you are righteous. That is the truth. Do not believe your thoughts but let us believe the truth.

Just as the blood of the lamb was put on the side doorposts and the upper doorpost, the blood has also been placed on the door of our heart. The blood that Jesus shed on the cross has washed our sins whiter than the snow. We have been made righteous and holy. I believe that when we believe the Bible, God will bless us.

Chapter 6

When You Put Away Your Thoughts and Believe the Word

When You Put Away Your Thoughts and Believe the Word

Jesus has done a lot of work in us for many years. Some things appear very difficult in the beginning, but God gave us so much grace and so many blessings, as if we were in a dream. This is especially true this time around—God had me overflow with great joy and thankfulness when I was preparing to preach this word. Today, we'll read from John chapter 3, verse 1 through 21:

> There was a man of the Pharisees, named Nicodemus, a ruler of the Jews: The same came to Jesus by night, and said unto him, Rabbi, we know that thou art a teacher come from God: for no man can do these miracles that thou doest, except God be with him.

Jesus answered and said unto him, Verily, verily, I say unto thee, Except a man be born again, he cannot see the kingdom of God. Nicodemus saith unto him, How can a man be born when he is old? can he enter the second time into his mother's womb, and be born? Jesus answered, Verily, verily, I say unto thee, Except a man be born of water and of the Spirit, he cannot enter into the kingdom of God. That which is born of the flesh is flesh; and that which is born of the Spirit is spirit. Marvel not that I said unto thee, Ye must be born again. The wind bloweth where it listeth, and thou hearest the sound thereof, but canst not tell whence it cometh, and whither it goeth: so is every one that is born of the Spirit. Nicodemus answered and said unto him, How can these things be? Jesus answered and said unto him, Art thou a master of Israel, and knowest not these things? Verily, verily, I say unto thee, We speak that we do know, and testify that we have seen; and ye receive not our witness. If I have told you earthly things, and ye believe not, how shall ye believe, if I tell you of heavenly things? And no man hath ascended up to heaven, but he that came down from heaven, even the Son of man which is in heaven. And as Moses lifted up the serpent in the wilderness, even so must the Son of man be lifted up: That whosoever believeth in him should not perish, but have eternal life. For God so loved the world, that he gave his only begotten Son, that whosoever believeth in him should not perish, but have everlasting life. For God sent not his Son into the world to condemn the world; but that the world through him might be saved. He that beleiveth on him is not condemned: but he that believeth not is condemned already, because he hath not believed in the name of the only begotten Son of God. And this is the condemnation, that light is come into the world, and men loved darkness rather than light, because their deeds were evil. For every one that doeth evil hateth the light, neither cometh to the light, lest his deeds should be reproved. But he that doeth truth cometh to the light, that his deeds may be made manifest, that they are wrought in God. (John 3:1-21)

Clara and Her Father's Tears

I'm so thankful we can hold this conference. I'm not exactly sure the amount, but this conference is going to be broadcasted on many TV stations around the world. I know that many people will be listening to the sermons. I cannot express just how thankful I am that I'm able to share the words and heart of Jesus, and not my own words.

In 2001, I founded an organization called International Youth Fellowship (IYF). At first glance, it appears that the youths of the world are led by many wrongful thoughts. However, if you look at Ephesians chapter 2, you will clearly see that the "prince of the power of the air," which is a particular force, is the one leading their hearts. In other words, the evil spirit leads people's hearts. Often times, young people fall into the pleasures of the flesh, their ambitions, and misery.

Once, we held an IYF World Camp in Mexico. Usually, these camps draw an attendance of thousands of young people. During IYF World Camp, the award-winning, internationally renowned Gracias Choir performs amazing music for attendees. And I give mind lectures during the camp. I speak about the world of the heart.

On the first night of the IYF World Camp in Mexico, right before I concluded my lecture, I asked all the students there, "Everyone, all of you have cellphones, right?"

They all simultaneously replied, "Yes, we do."

I made a request: "Once this lecture ends, go to a quiet place, and call your father. Say to him, 'Father, thank you very much. Father, you do so many things for our family. Sometimes, I just gloss over it, but I am aware of it. And so, today, I just want to thank you.' It's okay to tell him, 'Father, there are many people who live in difficulty without their fathers. However, because we have you, our family is strong and well.' If you feel too awkward saying this to your father, then you can speak to a coconut tree or a mango tree."

After the lecture was over, every student took their phones outside. The following morning, a sedan pulled into the camp. A middle-aged man got out of the car, and asked, "My daughter is attending this camp. Her name is Clara. I want to see her." The camp program had not started for the day, so we made a public announcement in order to locate Clara. The program manager who was running the camp sat and waited with the middle-aged man. Soon, a young girl came running from a distance.

She stood in front of her father, broke down, and cried out, "Father, I'm very sorry. I'm a terrible daughter. Please forgive me." Then her father held his daughter tightly in his arms, and she hugged her father tightly, too, and they cried together.

See, Clara had a boyfriend, and one day, he told her, "Clara, I need to show you something."

"What is it?" she asked.

Her boyfriend opened his bag, and Clara was shocked. The bag was filled with $100 bills. She asked him, "What's all this money?"

He answered, "Don't worry, I didn't steal it. It's money I've been saving up since I was a kid."

She asked him, "What are you going to do with it?"

"I want to move to Canada and live with you. Do you want to come with me?"

"Yes," she replied.

Clara was very happy about this, and not too long afterwards, the two of them were at the airport to board a flight for Canada. Clara's father also came to the airport, but he said, "Clara, you're too young to be doing this right now. You have plenty of time to do this after you graduate college. You need to be studying right now." Her father explained everything sincerely. However, Clara's heart was already completely filled with the notion of going to Canada with her boyfriend. She rejected her father's words and boarded the plane to Canada.

She liked being in Canada in the beginning. However, as time passed, things became more and more difficult. She enjoyed seeing her boyfriend from time to time before. However, now, they were together all of the time, and she ended up colliding with him in many ways.

Then one day, Clara had an argument with her boyfriend. He asked her, "Clara, you bought this again?"

"Well, we need it."

"We don't have much money left. What are we going to do if you keep spending money like this?"

"What's the point of having money if we're not going to buy what we need?"

"But we're low on money, so you need to conserve it."

The two of them became more and more uncomfortable with each other. The day came when Clara could no longer stay with her boyfriend. So, she boarded a plane and returned to Mexico. Her father got the news that his daughter was returning, so he went to the airport to pick her up.

Clara got off the airplane and was exiting the airport, when she saw her father waiting for her. She wanted to run to him and fall in his arms, saying, "Father!" However, on one side of her heart, she thought, "I disobeyed my father, and went to Canada." She felt so guilty that she was unable to face him. So, she hid and exited through a different door, and found her own way home.

It would have been so much better if she held her father's hands, came out of the airport, got in her father's car, and came home together. It would have been so nice. However, Clara did her father wrong in so many ways that she felt like she couldn't look him in the face anymore.

Every morning, she would stay in bed with her blanket over her head until her father went to work. She would only get out of bed after her father left. It was extremely difficult going through each day like this. That is when she attended IYF World Camp. And it just so happened that on the first evening, while listening to my lecture, she heard me tell everyone, "Call your fathers." That's when she had the heart, "I should do what the pastor is telling us to do." She actually called her father, saying, "Father, it's me, Clara. I've been terribly wrong, but it was too hard for me to apologize. Father, please forgive me."

After he received that phone call from his loving daughter, he couldn't sleep all night. As soon as the next day broke, he drove his car to the camp venue and his daughter. Clara said to him, "Father, I'm a bad daughter. I wanted to be good to you, but I've only done you wrong. Please forgive me." He hugged his daughter and cried. Clara also cried. They were able to recover their beautiful family.

How Can Our Hearts Flow with God?

This is also true between us and God. God wants to be close with us and get along with us. We are the ones who feel very guilty in front of Him because our hearts flow according to the desires of our flesh. However, there is something that God requests of us.

God does not request that we do something great, give lots of money as an offering, or put our life on the line for somebody else. He is not requesting anything like that.

God wants His heart to flow together with ours, just as Clara's father's heart flowed with Clara's heart. How can God's heart and our hearts flow together? It's very simple. All you have to do is hear the His word and accept it.

In John chapter 1, God said: *In the beginning was the word. And the word was with God and the word was God." (John 1:1)* It clearly says that the word, itself, is God. *"In the beginning was the Word, and the Word was with God, and the Word was God. The same was in the beginning with God. All things were made by him; and without him was not any thing made that was made. (John 1:1-3)* It says that all things were made by the word. And then the word came in the form of the flesh: *And the Word was made flesh, and dwelt among us, (and we beheld his glory, the glory as of the only begotten of the Father,) full of grace and truth. (John1:14)* However, in the previous verses, it says, *He came unto his own, and his own received him not. But as many as received him, to them gave he power to become the sons of God, even to them that believe on his name: (John 1:11-12)* This is the main message of the book of John.

Is there anybody who has the same heart as Jesus? Not one single person? What should we do, then? We just need to accept the word. How do we do that? All we have to do is just accept everything by faith even though we may not understand it. Those words will enter your heart and rule over it.

Jesus is the almighty God, therefore, He has a lot of methods, power, and wisdom. I'm human, and because I follow after my flesh, I could never reach the level of wisdom or power of Jesus. I cannot understand every word Jesus has spoken. But to be able to believe, we don't need to understand as much as the one speaking.

Suppose I go to a restaurant together with Pastor Joseph, who is translating. I say to him, "Pastor Joseph, what would you like to eat? The potato soup is really good. Would you like some?" In Korea, the potato soup is very tasty. I used to think that Korean potato soup was actually made with potatoes. However, the soup has very few potatoes. Instead, it has lots of pork attached to pig bones. The meat on those bones is very tasty. Those of you who get to visit Korea, please have some Korean potato soup. It may be a little bit burdensome if you are a foreigner, but you will enjoy it very much once you try it.

Suppose I tell Pastor Joseph, "Let's get some potato soup. Would you like some Korean potato soup?"

He asks, "What is Korean potato soup?"

"It's got potatoes, pork, and pig bones that are boiled together. The meat is very tasty. If you eat it, you will know what it is."

Then he answers, "Alright, I'll try it this one time." Even though he doesn't know everything about the food, he's going to eat it. People don't decide to try food they already know about and have eaten before.

"Have you ever had that dish?"

"What is it?"

"Would you like to try some?"

"Sure, can I have some? It's just food, how bad could it be?"

This is how you try and eat food. We don't understand

every word Jesus says. When you finally get to eat Korean potato soup, you can say, "So, this is what the Korean potato soup is," and you know what it is. It's really simple.

"Would you like to eat some Korean potato soup?"

"What is that?"

"It's a soup that boils potatoes with pig bones, with pork still on the bone. It's delicious."

"Alright, I'll try some."

Even though he's never had it before, he'll know the taste of the Korean potato soup once he eats it. This is true with all food. This is also how it is when it comes to accepting the words of Jesus into our hearts. It is the same as saying, "Alright, I'll receive it this time." Do not try to understand everything. Just simply go ahead and accept what Jesus says. And, often times, you'll understand after you've accepted His words. You'll have the same heart as Jesus—this is what it means to accept the words of Jesus.

The Spiritual Life Taught to Us by the Gospel of John

In John chapter 3, Nicodemus comes to see Jesus at night. Jesus says to Nicodemus, "Unless a man is born again, he cannot see the kingdom of heaven." Nicodemus tried to understand the words of Jesus, so he asks, "How could a man be born again? Can he enter a second time into his mother's womb, and then be birthed back out?" However, that's not what he should be doing. He should be accepting Jesus' words. It's all about saying, "Jesus, did you say, 'born again?' I don't know what it means to be born again, but I want to be born again. If you tell me to do so, then I'll go ahead and do it."

Nicodemus called Jesus a teacher from heaven. He mentions how nobody could do what Jesus has done unless God was with Him. However, even though Nicodemus said all of that, he couldn't accept the words Jesus gave him. Let's talk about this a little bit more.

The Gospel of John is a very interesting book. In chapter 3, Jesus continuously explained things to Nicodemus, but he is unable to comprehend anything at his own level. Therefore, their conversation just ends without any progress.

A different situation is described in chapter 4. The Samaritan woman had a conversation with Jesus. They were talking about water, but then Jesus said, *Whosoever drinketh of this water shall thirst again: But whosoever drinketh of the water that I shall give him shall never thrist; but the water that I shall give him shall be in him a well of water springing up into everlasting life. (John 4:13-14)*

Do you know what water Jesus is talking about when He said it is a water that would allow you to never thirst again? There's no way that we could possibly understand everything Jesus says since there's a difference in level between us and God. There's no one who can know the taste of Korean potato soup without actually having some. Even though a person may not know how it tastes, if they eat it one time, they will say, "Ah, this is the Korean potato soup. It's pretty good. Next time, I'm going to buy some for my friends." Then, that person will be able to enjoy Korean potato soup again another time.

Jesus said, "Whoever drinks of this water will thirst again. But whoever drinks the water I will give him, will never thirst." Water reminds me of the time I received ranger training in the army. We received the ranger training in the rugged mountains. We would do lots of calisthenics to warm up before training sessions. The trainer will shout out, "First, we'll do high jumps!" The trainer would do one rep, and then everyone else would do 999 reps to total 1,000 reps.

But on the last rep, you're not supposed to shout out the count. So, you have hundreds of soldiers doing high jumps together. They have to jump a thousand times. Each time, they jump, they would count out loud, "One! Two!" However, you cannot count out 1,000th rep out loud. So, after we jumped very hard and get to 999, many soldiers would grumble warnings to each other, saying, "Hey, don't say 1,000. Don't say 1,000." However, there would always be somebody who yelled out, "1,000!" Then, everyone had to start all over again. When that happens, it just sucks all the energy from your entire body. We would sweat so profusely. We filled our water canteens and drank them dry several times over, but we were always thirsty. But here, Jesus talks about the water that "will make you never thirst."

There is no water source that quenches your thirst with one drink, as far as we know. Does such water exist? It does not. However, the Samaritan woman listened to Jesus' words that she couldn't understand, and she responded in a very different way from Nicodemus.

Most would say, "Is there any kind of water like that in this entire world? Please don't joke with someone you're seeing for the first time." However, this was how the Samaritan woman responded, "Lord, give me this water that I thirst not neither come hither to draw." Nicodemus says that he knows Jesus was a teacher sent by God in heaven, but he refused His words.

Jesus never told us to do something. *He came unto his own, and his own received him not. But as many as received him, to them gave he power to become the sons of God, even to them that believe on his name. (John 1:11-12)* We just need to simply accept the words He has spoken. The words of Jesus are the truth, so we cannot understand every word. But it's about accepting it by faith, it's not about trying to understand it.

A man who had an infirmity for 38 years appears in John, chapter 5. There were lots of sick people gathered at the pool of Bethesda. And when the angel comes down and troubles the water, if you were the first one in, you would be healed of your disease. Many sick people waited for the water of the pool to be troubled so they could be healed. However, the man with the infirmity for 38 years was not poolside. He was at a place a little off from the pool because it didn't matter if he saw the angel troubling the water before anyone else—he was unable to move properly. He could never be the first person into the pool. Jesus met this man and asked him, "Wilt thou be made whole?"

He replied, "Lord, when the water is troubled, there's no man to put me into the pool. That as I go down, somebody else will go before me." The sick man spoke from his heart.

This was Jesus' reply: "Rise, take up thy bed and walk."

This is just like eating potato soup for the first time. This person had been sick and could not move properly for 38 years. Not once was there a time when he could get up and walk. The person who eats Korean potato soup for the first time will not know the taste. He or she just listens to the person with him and orders the food not knowing what it will taste like.

Jesus told this man, "Rise, take up your bed and walk." This was something he had never done before. He thought to himself, "I cannot make this work. But He is telling me to walk, so let me just try to get up and walk." Doing this is accepting the words Jesus has spoken.

When Jesus told the man to take up his bed and walk, the sick man must have thought deep inside, "I've wanted to walk so badly my entire life. I was never able to, and I cannot even properly lift my own body, even now. However, I will walk as you have said." This is the spiritual life that the Gospel of John is teaching.

The Word Is Not to Be Understood But Believed

Nicodemus was more than capable of having faith and not speaking according to his own thoughts, but saying, "Jesus, I really don't understand what you mean when you spoke about being born again. But I want to be born again. What should I do? I will do exactly what you tell me to do." Had he said that, Jesus would have taught him the way. However, Nicodemus spoke very negatively. So, Jesus explained to him in a little simpler way.

And as Moses lifted up the serpent in the wilderness, even so must the Song of man be lifted up: That whosoever believeth in him should not perish, but have eternal life. (John 3:14-15) Here, Jesus is talking about the words in Numbers chapter 21. The Israelites were walking in the wilderness, and they were discouraged in their hearts because of the way there. They blamed God, and God responded by sending fiery serpents. I heard that the fiery serpents could leap a meter at a time. The people were being bitten by the fiery serpents, and they were dying.

The Israelites eventually admitted they were wrong, and they asked God to get rid of the fiery serpents. Moses earnestly asked God to get rid of the fiery serpents, but God did not get rid of them. Instead, He told Moses to make a brass serpent and put it upon a pole. Then He said, "Whoever has been bitten and looks at the brass serpent will live."

These people were bitten by poisonous snakes and were about to die. To say, "If you look at a serpent made of brass, you will live," cannot be rationalized. However, this is not something that should be understood, but believed. Even though you don't understand what somebody is saying, you can accept their words if you trust them: "Oh, I don't understand this aspect. But this person is trustworthy." If you do accept those words, you will experience and understand everything.

We have to experience the things we've never experienced before in order to actually experience it. No one can experience something otherwise. You may not understand, but you will once you accept it. It is just like a person who doesn't know how to drive. Once that person turns the ignition on, and begins to drive, he or she is able to learn how. This is how people learn.

The same goes for learning faith. Even though you may not understand things, it's about accepting the words of Jesus. However, Nicodemus did not accept the words that Jesus said: "Just as Moses lifted up the serpent in the wilderness, so shall the son of man be lifted up." The serpent that Moses made was made of brass. Therefore, it is called the brass serpent in the Bible.

All the minerals in the Bible have meanings. Gold represents the glory of God. Silver represents the price of redemption. Brass represents judgment. And whenever God expressed judgment, He used brass. Moses put the brass serpent on a pole in the wilderness. The people were told that if the people who were bitten, looked at that brass serpent, they would live. *And the Lord said unto Moses, Make thee a fiery serpent, and set it upon a pole: and it shall come to pass, that every one that is bitten, when he looketh upon it, shall live. (Numbers. 21:8)*

Jesus told Nicodemus, *Just like the brass serpent was lifted up, the Son of man will also be lifted up.* This is so that whosoever believes in Him shall have everlasting life: *And as Moses lifted up the serpent in the wilderness, even so must the Son of man be lifted up: That whosoever believeth in him should not perish, but have eternal life. (John 3:14-15)* In reality, we can see the image of Jesus being lifted up as He was crucified, just like how the brass serpent was placed on a pole and lifted up. Why was Jesus nailed to the cross? He was crucified in our stead. He received God's judgment instead of us. The brass serpent in Numbers 21 represents Christ who was crucified.

When some people were bitten by the fiery serpents, the poison tormented them and killed them. In the same way, when we commit sin, the sin causes us pain and makes us receive destruction. While the children of Israel were being bitten by the fiery serpents and dying, God said, "Make a brass serpent and put it upon a pole. Then, whoever is bitten, will live when they look at the brass serpent." Among the children of Israel, there must have been people who thought, "We're being bitten by fiery serpents. Why should we look at the brass serpent? That does not make any sense." However, if you look in the Bible, it says, *And Moses made a serpent of brass, and put it upon a pole, and it came to pass, that if a serpent had bitten any man, when he beheld the serpent of brass, he lived. (Numbers 21:9).* The Bible portrays the brass serpent as Jesus Christ, who was meant to receive judgment for our sins. That's why we look to Jesus, who was crucified on the cross.

Why did Jesus put on the crown of thorns? Why was He wounded? Why did He shed His blood? He received the punishment of our sins instead of us. "Ah, Jesus received the punishment for my sins. If that's the case, it means all my sins have been washed away. That means I am clean. The judgment that Jesus received was the judgment for my sins. And because Jesus received the judgment I was supposed to accept, there is no more judgment remaining for me to receive." I believed in this truth.

In Romans chapter 3, verse 23, it says, *For all have sinned and come short of the glory of God.* But in verse 24 it says, ... *through the redemption that is in Christ Jesus.* Jesus redeemed us. What did He do? The judgment that we were supposed to receive for our sins, Jesus accepted instead. Therefore, Jesus was crucified, receiving the judgment for our sins.

I stole, I lied, and I committed many sins. However, the judgment for all those sins was finished on the cross. When we look at the cross, we can know, "That's where the judgment for my sins has ended. It ended there. All my sins are washed." We become free from God's judgment when we have faith. Jesus shed His blood, His forehead was torn, and his hands and feet were nailed. He received the complete judgment for all man's sins, which is what every one of us were supposed to suffer. The judgment for our sins ended there, and so, our sins have all been washed away. Hallelujah!

People Who Still Say That They're Sinners

Many people who go to church today say they are sinners even though they also say Jesus died on the cross for their sins. If they're sinners even though they believe in Jesus, what impact did the death of Jesus have on us? What does the crucifixion of Jesus have to do with you if it can't wash away your sins? Jesus was not crucified because He had sins. He received the punishment for our sins in our place.

I'll explain it like this: Suppose I lied, stole something, and committed many other sins. Then, I went to trial. When I get to court, they read the record of all the sins I committed. I would think, "Wow, I committed lots of sins. It's going to be scary to receive the punishment for all of them." However, it is also recorded in the legal document that Jesus would receive the punishments I was supposed to receive.

If Jesus had received every punishment for every single sin I committed, that means they are all finished. However, so many churches teach people that they are still sinners. Those pastors say that they are sinners, elders say that they are sinners. If that's true, then what is the point of Jesus being crucified?

Who was delivered for our offences, and was raised again for our justification. (Romans 4:25) Here, it says that Jesus was delivered for our offenses, and He was raised again for our justification. If we are righteous and if we are just, that means that all of our sins have been forgiven and washed away. We are without sins because all our sins have been washed away. And that's why God says we are righteous.

The people who say that they believe in Jesus, but also say they are still a sinner are basically saying that

Jesus' death on the cross was vain. People call themselves sinners because they have committed sins. However, you having committed sins is not the only factor to consider. Jesus has washed all those sins away. To believe in Jesus is to believe that all our sins have been washed at the cross. If we are still sinners, it means our sins have not been washed away despite Jesus being crucified. That cannot be faith.

God's thoughts are different from our thoughts. People do not give their lives for others. But God gave His son's life for us. If Jesus was crucified, then our sins have been washed. That was the reason Jesus traveled that whole path in the first place. Even though he was crucified, if people are still sinners, then why would Jesus walk the path He walked? Jesus was crucified on the cross, and He washed away all our sins.

Jeremiah chapter 31, verse 34 tells us, ... *saith the LORD: for I will forgive their iniquity, and I will remember their sin no more.* Clara did a lot of wrong by her father, but he truly loved his daughter. When he heard that his daughter was returning to Mexico from Canada, he was so happy that he went to pick her up at the airport. However, Clara saw her father waiting for her. She wanted to fall into his arms and cry out, "Father!" But that's when she remembered everything she had done wrong. And so, she just hid. Her father actually went to the airport with a heart that had already forgiven every one of her wrongdoings. However, Clara did not know he had that heart.

When Clara attended the IYF World Camp, she listened

to my lecture and called her father. After receiving her phone call, her father couldn't sleep, he was so happy. As soon as day broke, he jumped in his car and rushed to our IYF World Camp. Clara told her father, "Father, I'm so sorry." Because her father loved Clara, he did not want to blame her. He only wanted his heart to flow with his daughter's heart. So, when Clara said, "Father, I'm so sorry," everything ended right then and there.

Every one of us has committed sins. We have done wrong, and God knows us. He knows that we could only commit sin. Therefore, God sent Jesus to this world in order to wash our sins away. Jesus washed away all of our sins and made us as white as snow. However, the same way Clara did not return to her father, there are people who hold onto their own thoughts and continue to call themselves sinners because they are deceived by Satan. They are rebelling against Jesus, who hung on the cross for them.

Even though the Samaritan woman did not understand what Jesus was saying when He said, "Whosoever drinks of this water shall thirst again, but whosoever drinks the water that I give him shall never thirst," she simply accepted them.

The man who had an infirmity for 38 years knew very clearly that he could not walk. However, he walked. Before he met Jesus, he could not walk, no matter how hard he tried. However, when Jesus said, "Rise, take up your bed, and walk," the man thought to himself, "Wow, He's telling me to walk, so, His words must be correct. Let's walk," and he stood up and walked. I too, simply accepted the Word of God that said, "I will forgive their iniquity, and remember their sins no more." God forgave all of my sins, and He has said that He remembers my sins no more. And God does not lie. If God did remember our sins, then how shameful would it be for me every time I stand in front of God? I, too, would have to avoid God like Clara did to her father.

However, all we have to do is to simply accept the words, "… saith the Lord: for I will forgive their iniquity, and I will remember their sin no more." All we have to do is simply accept these words as they are. There's nothing to discuss. There's nothing to research. We should all just have the heart, "Wow, God is saying that my sins have been forgiven. Then, my sins are forgiven. He has promised that He remembers my sins no more." That is all how we need to be. It's simple: we just need to accept the Word of God, which is different from our state.

Now, in Isaiah chapter 55, verse 8, the Bible says, *For my thoughts are not your thoughts, neither are your ways my ways, saith the Lord.* God's thoughts and our thoughts are completely different. God loves us. He's the one who saved us.

I have committed many sins, and I have often felt guilty in my conscience. Quite simply put, I believe God has forgiven my sins and remembers them no more. From the moment I believed, God entered my heart and worked in my life. As a result, my heart was connected with God's heart, and God has been leading me ever since. God leads us to new, unimaginable ways. It is so amazing, and I am very thankful.

Because Clara's father loved her, he forgave everything she did. But the problem was that Clara closed her heart and did not speak to him. Likewise, God has already washed all of our sins away, so do not think that you're a sinner. Do not believe in your thoughts. Instead, believe the Word of God. Although you may vividly remember all the sins you've committed, proclaim the truth that these sins have all been washed. Accept the Word of God into your heart that assures us that Jesus has cleansed us of our sins. Go ahead and accept the God's promise that He truly remembers our sins, no more. Then, your heart will become bright, you'll become happy, and the Holy Spirit will be upon you.

Satan will try to block this, but don't be deceived by him. Whatever sin it may have been, it was taken care of on the cross. After Clara's father and Clara met at the World Camp venue, the two of them were able to live together in peace. When I returned to Mexico later, I heard that Clara was getting married. I believe that family will live in happiness even now.

Even Though You Don't Understand, if You Accept It as It Is...

You cannot deliver man from sin with the love of man. God has such a great love man can never fully fathom. For that reason, alone, don't try to understand the Word of God. Just believe it. Even though I cannot walk, if Jesus tells me to walk, then I need go ahead and walk. If Jesus says that we are washed, then we need to believe we've been washed. If God says that He remembers your sins no more, just believe it. That's what it means to believe in Jesus. Believing in Jesus is accepting the words of Jesus, exactly as they are written, not hearing the words of Jesus, and then living according to your own thoughts.

For all have sinned, and come short of the glory of God; Being justified by his grace through the redemption that is in Christ Jesus. (Romans 3:23-24) Jesus redeemed us. He paid the price for the sins we have committed in our place, and He delivered us from sin. We have been justified freely by the grace of God. God tells us that we are justified. Then, are we still going to say we are sinners? You're an enemy to Jesus if that's the case.

I may not know much, but if Jesus says that I am justified, then I am righteous, despite the fact that I have committed many, many sins. This is what it means to believe Jesus. If you believe, then you become free from sin. You don't need to pray on a mountain to wash away your sins. You don't need to pray all night long, either. Actually, you don't have to do anything. It truly looks like I am a sinner, as far as my thoughts go. However, Jesus tells me that I'm righteous. He is telling us that He has washed away all our sins, as white as snow. If that is the case, then even though it may feel as if I still have sins, the truth is that they have all been washed away. Believing this way, is to truly believe in Jesus.

Do not exalt your thoughts to be higher than Jesus' words. No matter what your thoughts may be, believe the Word of God. Then, your heart will be connected with God's heart in an amazing way. From that moment on, God will lead you, and so will the Holy Spirit. Even though you may have been led by the evil spirit and lived a lustful and evil life, if you are led by the Holy Spirit, your life will inevitably change.

Live with the thoughts and heart of Jesus. When your thoughts and Jesus' thoughts differ, do not accept your own. Accept the words of Jesus. The heart that you need to have is, "I think and believe that I cannot walk. However, Jesus told me to walk, so I'm going to walk. I think that I'm a sinner, but if Jesus says I'm justified, that means I am righteous."

In 1962, I discovered that my sins were forgiven in the Bible. 2022 will mark 60 years since I was born again. And it's not because I have had a particularly special experience. It's just that the Bible told me that my sins have been washed away. It says that God remembers my sins no more, and my sins have been washed clean, so I have become holy.

Hebrews chapter 10, verse 10 says, *By the which will we are sanctified through the offering of the body of Jesus Christ once for all.* Not only did God make me holy, He has perfected me forever. Of course, the reality of, "I am perfect forever," is something God accomplished. When you first eat Korean potato soup, you are unfamiliar with it. But, you can acquire the taste once you eat it. And you'll want to eat it again since it's not that expensive.

When I first read the words in the Bible that are about Jesus, everything was so unfamiliar because those words were different from my thoughts. I thought that I was a sinner, but Jesus said that I was righteous. Right then, I threw my thoughts away, and I decided to believe in the words of Jesus. Everyone, throw away your thoughts, and look to Jesus, who was hung on the cross. Then say this out loud, "Just like the brass serpent that was lifted up in the wilderness, Jesus was crucified on the cross. He was lifted up, and received all the judgment for our sin, which we were all supposed to be accountable for. All my sins have been finished." Live this way. The Holy Spirit of God will be upon you, and you will experience amazing change.

Chapter 7

The King's Minister, Who Was Unable to Believe the Word of God

The King's Minister, Who Was Unable to Believe the Word of God

It's so amazing that we can share the heart of God, as we enter into the world of God with an open Bible right in front of us. There is no other way we could ever come to know the heart of God apart from the Bible.

A long time ago, it was very hard to get a Bible, but now, it is very easy to get your hands on one. So, I have a Bible in my bedroom, and one in my office. I keep my Bibles there, and I read them often. We will read from 2 Kings chapter 7, starting from verse 1:

Then Elisha said, Hear ye the word of the Lord; Thus saith the Lord, To morrow about this time shall a measure of fine flour be sold for a shekel, and two

measures of barley for a shekel, in the gate of Samaria.
Then a lord on whose hand the king leaned answered
the man of God, and said, Behold, if the Lord would
make windows in heaven, might this thing be? And
he said, Behold, thou shalt see it with thine eyes, but
shalt not eat thereof. And there were four leprous men
at the entering in of the gate: and they said one to
another, Why sit we here until we die? If we say, We
will enter into the city, then the famine is in the city,
and we shall die there: and if we sit still here, we die
also. Now therefore come, and let us fall unto the host
of the Syrians: if they save us alive, we shall live; and
if they kill us, we shall but die. And they rose up in the
twilight, to go unto the camp of the Syrians: and when
they were come to the uttermost part of the camp of
Syria, behold, there was no man there. For the Lord
had made the host of the Syrians to hear a noise of
chariots, and a noise of horses, even the noise of a
great host: and they said one to another, Lo, the king
of Israel hath hired against us the kings of the Hittites,
and the kings of the Egyptians, to come upon us.
Wherefore they arose and fled in the twilight, and left
their tents, and their horses, and their asses, even the
camp as it was, and fled for their life. And when these
lepers came to the uttermost part of the camp, they
went into one tent, and did eat and drink, and carried
thence silver, and gold, and raiment, and went and hid
it; and came again, and entered into another tent, and
carried thence also, and went and hid it. Then they
said one to another, We do not well: this day is a day

of good tidings, and we hold our peace: if we tarry till
the morning light, some mischief will come upon us:
now therefore come, that we may go and tell the king's
household. So they came and called unto the porter
of the city: and they told them, saying, We came to the
camp of the Syrians, and, behold, there was no man
there, neither voice of man, but horses tied, and asses
tied, and the tents as they were. (2 Kings 7:1-10)

The Bible is the Word of God. If you look inside of the Bible, the precise heart of God lies within its pages. When we accept the words of God into our hearts, we are able to have a heart that is the same as God's heart. And then, God works with power inside of that person.

While you read the Bible, God wants you to accept the words in the Bible as His words. God wants us to accept His word and throw away all the thoughts we have. When you accept it, your heart becomes one with the heart of God. Then the heart of God that you did not have before works inside of you—you are changed into a whole new person.

If God Were to Make Windows in Heaven, Might These Things Be?

A long time ago, there was a war between Israel and Syria. Syria was invading Israel, so the two nations fought. When Israel was about to lose, the people fled into the city walls, and locked the city gates. The Syrian soldiers set up camp a short distance away from the city and waited for the Israelites to surrender. The people of

Israel were unable to come outside of the city walls.

I heard that the Japanese only built walls around the king's palace. Korean people built walls around the city. The Chinese built a wall around the entire country. When you build a wall around the whole country like China did, you can farm and live inside the walls. However, most cultures would only build walls around settled areas. This prohibited people from being able to reach the farmlands. Eventually, you would naturally run out of food.

As time passed, the people who fled to the city started to grow hungry. I read from 2 Kings chapter 7, verse 1. Towards the end of chapter 6, it talks about how two women boiled and ate one of their own children. If a person becomes very hungry, then that person becomes mentally ill. That person's heart changes, and he or she becomes capable of boiling and eating people. The city of Samaria was nearing destruction.

When we are inside of suffering or despair, God is our help. When we read the Word of God in times like these, we can become freed from any problem. However, even though the word of power is in our midst, the word becomes powerless if we do not accept them.

Samaria was running out of food. The people would soon die, one by one, in that situation. Right then, Elisha, the man of God, said, "Everyone, listen to the word of the Lord. The Lord says that tomorrow about this time, at the gates of Samaria a measure of fine flour will be sold for a shekel, and two measures of barley for a shekel."

The people thought to themselves, "What? A shekel for a measure of fine flour and two measures of barely? Are you telling me that food is going to be that cheap? That's so nice to hear. I really hope it will turn out that way."

However, right then, one of the king's ministers stood up and said, "That's nonsense. Even if God were to make windows in heaven, how could such a thing happen?" What was the difference between the minister and the people? The people received hope in their hearts when they listened to the words of Elisha. They said, "Tomorrow about this time, we'll be able to get food at cheap prices. How could this happen? Even just hearing about it has made me so happy. It would be so wonderful if this actually happens. Then we will not die." However, the minister laughed and said that it was nonsense.

What the Bible is telling us is the difference between the Word of God and our thoughts. The thoughts that we originally have are influenced very heavily by Satan. The prince of the power of the air, Satan, continues to work in our hearts and makes us stray further and further away from God. That's why the heart we have is not like the Word of God. Whoever wants to live a proper spiritual life must read the Bible. Genesis, Exodus, Leviticus, Deuteronomy...when you read the Bible, it is the Word of God no matter how it looks in your eyes. God does not lie. Therefore, everything will happen according to God's words. When you believe so, God works amazingly.

John Choi, Who Overcome the Poison of the Scorpion Through Strength from God

International Youth Fellowship works for the youth,

and we send hundreds of college students to many countries for a year of volunteer service annually. I've spoken about this story many times. A few years ago, a student named John Choi, who hails from Dallas, Texas, went to the country of Liberia in Africa to serve as a volunteer. One night, John was sleeping, but it was so hot that he opened the window and slept under a mosquito net. However, as he slept, his foot came out from inside the mosquito net. Right then, he felt a pain, as if someone took a needle and poked his foot.

"Ouch!" he cried out and he woke up. He looked around to see who it was, but there was no one there. So, he thought, "What was that?" and then fell back to sleep.

When he woke up the next morning, John Choi told the other volunteers who were next to him, "Hey, last night while I was sleeping, it felt like somebody stabbed my foot with a needle."

One of the volunteers answered, "Hey, maybe it was a scorpion."

John Choi said, "Hey, don't joke about that. There's no scorpion in our room."

He didn't think much about it, and just went about his day. But in the afternoon, he felt nauseated, and he collapsed on the way to the bathroom. The other members around him were shocked, and they ran over to him. He urinated and defecated in his pants, and couldn't breathe. He was dying. They quickly washed him and rushed him to the hospital. However, the doctor refused them and told them to take him away.

The doctor said, "This young man is dead. Take him away."

The director of IYF in Liberia begged the doctor, "Please help us."

"No. This young man has been stung by a scorpion. Even if you had brought him immediately after he was stung, he'd still barely have a chance. But right now, the poison of the scorpion has spread throughout his entire body. The poison has even reached his heart. There is no way to save him. He is going to die, so take him away."

They brought John Choi out from that hospital and went to another for help. However, that doctor said the same thing as the doctor of the previous hospital. At the next hospital, they begged and begged the doctor there, so he agreed to allow him to lay down on a hospital bed.

Not long afterwards, John Choi stopped breathing. They performed CPR to get his heart beating again, but he was dying. The doctor said there was no chance John Choi would survive. The Liberian branch director of IYF was crying when he called me on the phone.

He told me, "Pastor, do you know John Choi? John Choi!"

"Hey come on, what's wrong? Just calm down! Calm down. What's going on?"

"Yes, sorry, Pastor, I will be calm." Then he told me how John Choi was stung by a scorpion and that he was dying.

It takes 18 hours to travel from Seoul to Liberia on a plane. Could I send him medicine or a doctor? They said he was going to die in a few hours. Right then, a Bible verse came to mind: *"But they that wait upon the Lord shall renew their strength; they shall mount up with wings as eagles; they shall run, and not be weary; and they shall walk, and not faint." (Isaiah 40:31)*

"Can I speak to John on the phone?"

"Yes, Pastor," he answered. Then he handed the phone to John Choi and said, "John, it's Pastor Park."

So, I asked him, "John, can you hear my voice?"

John replied, "Yes, Pastor."

"They say you were stung by an African scorpion and that you're dying. However, this morning, I read Isaiah chapter 40, verse 31. It says, *They that wait upon the Lord shall renew their strength; they shall mount up with wings as eagles; they shall run, and not be weary; and they shall walk, and not faint.* John, all 66 books of the Bible are the words of God. God never ever lies. In order for you to overcome the scorpion's poison, you need new strength. Look to God and wait upon Him. Look to God. God says, 'But they that wait upon the Lord shall renew their strength.' The 66 books of the Bible are the words of God. Man should not be arguing about this or that with the Word of God. People must accept the words of God by faith. John, this is the Word of God. If you wait and look to the Lord, He will surely give you new strength."

I spoke to him for 15 minutes and then I asked him, "Do you believe this?"

John responded, "Yes, Pastor." Then, I hung up the phone. After that, I called the pastor of the Good News Dallas Church in Texas. I told him to call the brothers and sisters of the Dallas church and ask them to pray for John Choi. I told him to also tell John Choi's parents that he has been stung by a scorpion.

John Choi thought that he was going to die soon. However, hearing the words, "Wait upon the Lord," gave him the faith that he would gain new strength if he did just that, so he began to wait upon God. He prayed, "God, I will wait upon you. God, give me new strength." Then, he fell asleep.

Early in the morning, the nurse was dozing off, thinking, "Oh, that young man stung by the scorpion yesterday must be dead by now." Then she started to walk to the hospital room John Choi was in. When the nurse entered the hospital room, she was shocked. The night before, his body temperature was 18 degrees Celsius, and his blood pressure was at 20. He was essentially a corpse at that point. However, now his blood pressure was rising.

The nurse went to the doctor on duty and shouted, "Doctor! A miracle has happened to that young man stung by the scorpion!"

The doctor went to the hospital room and saw that his blood pressure was indeed rising. The doctor said, "Nurse, what did you do to this young man? How could this happen?"

The nurse replied, "I didn't do anything."

Later that morning, John Choi woke up. Everyone asked John, "Hey, are you okay?"

He replied, "Yes, I'm okay."

Then they said, "Hey, do you know what happened yesterday? You defecated and urinated in your pants. We had to wash you and bring you to the hospital."

Even though John Choi came back to life, the foot that was stung by the scorpion had already started to rot. But, his dead foot was completely healed after a month or two. He is now married and has become a father of three. He is living in so much happiness. The more I think about it, I am so thankful.

It's all about us looking up to God and believing what God has promised. God is not human. He does not say vain words. God keeps every word He has spoken to the letter. Therefore, if you hear the Word of God and accept it by faith, then the works of God will happen as promised.

Besides the incident with John Choi, I have experienced God working many, many times. I have personally experienced the works of God many times. I have also seen how God worked in people around me so many times. What does the Bible say? It says, "… they that wait upon the Lord shall renew their strength." There are many other words besides that. Whatever words they may be, the works of God happen when you believe them. Unfortunately, people are deceived by Satan, who tells them, "This is nonsense, how could these things happen?" Then they judge and distrust the words of God with their own thoughts. That's why they're unable to experience His words. The words of God will work as written when we read, hear, and believe in them.

The Decision of the Four Lepers: "Let's Go to the Syrian Camp"

In 2 Kings chapter 7, the city of Samaria was sieged and surrounded by Syrian soldiers. The people inside the city walls were starving to death. They would have caught rats and eaten them if that were possible. Some women even boiled and ate their own children.

God always gives us hope, though. So, one day, the man of God, Elisha, shouted out loud, "Everyone, hear the word of the Lord! In the word of the Lord has said that tomorrow about this time, a measure of fine flour will be sold for a shekel. And two measures of barely will be sold for a shekel in the gates of Samaria." It does not say in the Bible whether a measure of barely originally cost 5,000 or 10,000 shekels. Either way, these prices meant food was going to be extremely cheap.

A minister of the king, who heard this, said, "Even if God were to make windows in heaven, how could these things be?" That is not looking through the judgment of God, but through the judgment of man.

If it were just people who said that food would become cheap, then there is a chance that it may come true. On the other hand, if they are words that the man of God is saying, claiming them to be the Word of God, it will surely be achieved. However, this minister judged the Word of God with his own thoughts, and said, "How could such things happen?" Then the Prophet Elisha told him, "You shall see it with your own eyes, but you shall not eat thereof."

Now, let's take a look in the Bible to see how God worked afterwards. In verse 3 it says, *And there were four leprous men at the entering in of the gate: and they said one to another, Why sit we here until we die?* There were four lepers just outside the entrance of the gate. Lepers don't actually live at the entrance of a city's gate, but in a leper's colony.

Before the war, the lepers' families would bring food to them, and they would eat and live off of that. However, since the city gates were closed, and no one was bringing any food to the leper colonies, they were leaving their confines, one by one. This is how they arrived, step by step, at the entrance of the gate of Samaria.

Because the gate was locked, they were unable to enter the city. They just waited in front of the gate, hoping that their families would bring them some food. However, Samarians were starving to death and eating their own children in the city. Who could give the lepers any food? But they were still waiting outside with no hope. They told themselves, "Maybe today somebody will bring us some food. It would be great if someone would bring us some food."

Because they were hungry, the lepers would just sit there and talk about the past. "I remember the food I used to eat on my birthday a long time ago." Then, one of the lepers said, "Even though we sit here, nobody is going to bring us any food. How can we just sit here and wait to die?" God gave wisdom to these lepers, who were vaguely waiting for scraps of food. They began to have different thoughts. "Even if we could enter the city, the people there are starving. So, we will die there. If we stay here, we will also die. Let's go surrender to the Syrian camp. If they let us live, then we'll live. If we die, we die."

The four lepers did not go in the daytime since the weather was hot. Instead, they went towards the Syrian camp in the twilight. Walking was not easy because they were so hungry. They collapsed several times along the way.

One of them said, "I don't think I'm going to make it. Why don't you guys just leave me here? You guys go ahead and eat all the food."

"Hey, what are you talking about?" they replied. "We came here together. So, let's all go together. Get up. Let's be strong. Let's go."

As the day grew darker, they were unable to see in front of them. However, God did something amazing while the four lepers were stumbling and collapsing on the way to the Syrian camp. God made the sound of their footsteps like horses, chariot wheels, and a great army.

To the Syrian soldiers, the four lepers sounded like a huge marching army. "What is that sound? The king of Israel must have paid the Egyptian Pharaoh money and hired many soldiers to attack us." The sun was setting, and they were unable to see very well, but they heard tremendous sounds. The Syrian soldiers were completely shocked. They were inside of their tents boiling soup and were ready to eat dinner, they just ran away as fast as they could without looking back.

The lepers finally arrived at the Syrian camp, and shouted out, "Do not kill us! We surrender. Please, do not kill us!" However, it was complete silence. Something felt very strange, so they approached closer to the entrance of the camp. "Is anybody there?" they cried out, opening all the tents. The place was empty. There was only abandoned food still boiling and cooking. They told one another, "Whatever happens, let's eat first," and they mindlessly ate all the food they could stomach.

After they were full, they looked around the tent and found gold and silver. Then they began to hide everything. And they took everything in the other tents as well. The lepers said amongst themselves, "We do not well. This is a day of good tidings, but we are holding our peace. There is so much food here, so let us go tell the city of Samaria about this."

When the people of the city of Samaria were hungry, the man of God said this: *Then Elisha said, Hear ye the word of the Lord; Thus saith the Lord, Tomorrow about this time shall a measure of fine flour be sold for a shekel, and two measures of barley for a shekel, in the gate of Samaria. (2 Kings 7:1)* After hearing those words, one of the king's ministers said, "Behold, if the Lord would make windows in heaven, might this thing be?" This person did not believe in God as God, but as another human being. The man of God told him, "Behold, thou shalt see it with thine eyes, but shalt not eat thereof."

Time passed, and when the promised "tomorrow about this time" had arrived, a measure of fine flour was actually sold for a shekel, and two measures of barley were sold for a shekel. The important thing is that they were not treating God as God. If man says it, you can deem it impossible. However, is there anything God cannot do? He could do it tomorrow about this time, and of course, it could be done. However, the minister had his own thoughts, and calculated whether it was possible or impossible, himself. In his own eyes, it was impossible that a measure of fine flour would be sold for a shekel and two measures of barely for a shekel tomorrow about this time.

That is the same problem with our spiritual lives. With the same situation in front of us, the thoughts of man and the thoughts of God are different. If the people of the city of Samaria have no food, then they have no food. However, even though there is no food in the city, God is able to prepare more than enough food for the people inside Samaria to be able to eat, be full, and have leftovers.

God is not a poor person, nor is He a pathetic human being. He is God. If God has spoken it, it's okay, no matter how impossible it may seem in our eyes. Even though we cannot do it, God can do it. That is why we shouldn't follow our own judgment. My judgment may say it is impossible. However, God is able to do anything. You must have that faith. Then God lives and works inside of you.

Mr. Park, I Just Want to Live One Year with You

God did a lot of work in my life. After I was discharged from the army in 1968, I wanted to preach the gospel in the city of Gimcheon. At that time, I had about three dollars to my name. I had just been discharged from the army, and I did not know how much things cost at that time. With that money, I rode the train and went to Gimcheon. I arrived in Gimcheon, and I found a nice place to live. I asked how much it was going to be, and they asked for $70 dollars. The money I had was less than 1/20th of the cost of that place. I still remember it vividly.

That day, as I walked the streets of Gimcheon, I spoke to God in my heart. "God, look, there is a café over here. There is a tailor shop over there. And there's a bookstore. Even the god of this world gives his people buildings, but I'm a man of God. Will you not give me a house? Please give me a house." I looked all over Gimcheon, and then went back to Apkokdong where I was staying before. While in Apkokdong, I believed God would give me a house. I would occasionally go back to Gimcheon to look for a place to live.

Once, after looking for a place in Gimcheon, I was on the bus to go back to the city of Geochang. A foreigner sat next to me, and I asked him, "What country are you from?"

He replied, "I'm from England."

"What do you do?" I asked.

He replied, "I'm a missionary."

"Wow, you're doing great work. So, where are you going right now?"

"I'm travelling."

"Are you on a mission trip?"

"No, I'm just traveling."

When I heard that, I got angry, and said, "You're a missionary, and you're just traveling without preaching the gospel? You're a corrupt missionary."

His Korean-speaking ability and my English-speaking ability were similar, so I yelled at him with my nonsensical and broken English. However, the

Englishman was such a gentleman. He did not say anything and just listened to what I was saying.

Then the bus arrived at Geochang. I stood in line at the ticket booth to buy a ticket to go to Apkokdong.

The missionary walked up to me and said, "Mr. Park, could I spend a night at your house tonight?"

I answered, "Sure, come."

I went along with him to Apkokdong. Apkokdong is a village deep in the mountains without running water or a well. We lived drinking water from the creek, but the water was very fresh, so it was not a problem. However, the missionary drank from the creek water and began to have stomach pain. He needed to go to the bathroom all night long. I really felt bad. So, after that, I began to boil the water and give it to him. The missionary was bedridden for four days.

On the fourth day, the missionary finally got out of bed. He said, "Today, I will be going home."

I told him, "I'm really sorry."

"Mr. Park, there is something I want to tell you."

"What is it?"

"I'd like to live one year with you."

"Why do you want to live with me?"

"I've met many pastors and missionaries, but I've never met anyone who lives like you. I would like to learn how to live like you."

I laughed. I could not understand what there was to learn from my lifestyle. I told him, "No."

He asked, "Why not?"

"No one helps me. That is why I go hungry a lot." Back

then, I often experienced hunger. "I'm sure you're able to buy plenty of bread since you're a missionary who gets mission funding. If that's the case, I will look to you since you have bread and I am without bread. I'm afraid that you will offer me some bread. I want to receive everything from God. I'll let you stay if you promise me just one thing."

"What is that?" he asked.

"Even if I starve to death, you must not give me any bread. No matter what difficulties you have, I will not give you any money. If you are able to do that, then we can live together."

"Sure, I can do that without any problems."

"Alright then. I'll be working in Gimcheon in the future, so please find a place to live in Gimcheon for yourself."

The missionary agreed, and left Apkokdong. His name was Anderson.

Ten days later, Missionary Anderson came back to Apkokdong and said, "Mr. Park, I've been praying for Gimcheon, and God gave me money to buy a house there. Let's buy a place in Gimcheon with this money and live together." Upon hearing what the missionary said, I thought to myself, "Am I receiving the help of man?" However, I had the heart that this was how God was giving us a house in Gimcheon. So, we got a place in Gimcheon and lived together.

God has filled my every need in life until this point. Each time God worked for me, I was so thankful. Back then, life was difficult, and I often endured hunger. But these days, the books that I've written sell very well, and

I'm able to live without much difficulty. God has helped me with so many things, I could talk about it all night long and it wouldn't be enough time.

Believing the Word of God Is Believing God

Let's continue to talk about how God worked in 2 Kings chapter 7. Right now, God is also working. "Tomorrow about this time shall a measure of fine flour be sold for a shekel, and two measures of barley for a shekel." According to the Word of God, the four lepers said to each other, "If we stay here, we'll die. If we enter into the city, we'll die. There is no food anywhere. If we sit here, we will ultimately die. What's the point of us just waiting here to die? Let's surrender to the Syrian camp. There's lots of food at the camp. If they kill us, we'll just die. But if they let us live, we'll live. Let's at least get a look at the food."

That was the wisdom God gave the four lepers. The really amazing thing is that we are unable to believe the Word of God through our thoughts. God promised, "Tomorrow about this time, Samaria will overflow with food." However, the minister of the king thought, "In this situation, we are surrounded by Syrian soldiers. How could we ever get that much food? This is nonsense."

I, too, attended church for a long time, but was unable to believe in God. I tried hard to do good deeds and serve God. I accepted things that seemed possible to me, but I couldn't believe the things I considered impossible. I was similar with the king's minister who did not trust the

Word of God.

We learn about God through the Bible. It may look impossible in our eyes, but God is more than capable—when we believe in the Word of God, we become blessed. In Romans chapter 3, verses 23 and 24 say, *For all have sinned, and come short of the glory of God; Being justified freely by his grace through the redemption that is in Christ Jesus.* The Bible tells us that we are justified. Who is saying that we are justified? If the Bible says that we are justified, God is saying we are justified. That means we have actually been made righteous. However, I used to think that I had lots of sins because I stole, lied, and committed many sins, even though Jesus was crucified. That was the thought I had, so I always said I was a sinner.

The same way that the king's minister said it was nonsense when the man of God said the city of Samaria was going to overflow with food, God said I was justified, but I thought that was nonsense. Then, one day, the scriptures entered my heart, differently. I read Romans chapter 3, verse 23, which says, *For all have sinned, and come short of the glory of God.* Those words were just like my own heart: "That's right. I have committed sin, too." But verse 24 was saying completely the opposite: *Being justified freely by his grace through the redemption that is in Christ Jesus.* God was telling me that I was justified.

Jesus was crucified and paid the complete price for our sins, and because He saved us, God is telling us that we've been justified. God has made us righteous, freely, by His grace. So, what should we do? We must believe the Word of God. God tells me I'm justified. Even though every person has sinned, it is by the good work of Jesus that God tells me I'm righteous. He says that all my sins have been washed clean. That is how we should believe.

In the past, I believed in my circumstances just like the minister of the king. I thought, "How can I be righteous? I committed so many sins." That is why I had to pray for forgiveness, begging and repenting for my sins every day. After I read Romans chapter 3, verse 24, I was able to believe the fact that I have been made righteous.

Even though we have surely committed sins, God says that we're justified. In the city of Samaria there was absolutely no food, but God proclaimed that Samaria would overflow with food. The important factor is the one saying the words. Is it a pastor? Is it an elder? No. It was God. If God said, "Tomorrow about this time, the city of Samaria will overflow with food," then it will be done. If God says we're righteous, it doesn't matter what sins we may have committed, He's right. I'm righteous. God is not human. He is God, and God does not lie. That's why I am righteous if God says I'm justified, no matter the sins I may have committed. That's what it means to believe God.

When you believe in your own thoughts, you would say, "I have so many sins. How could I be righteous? That's nonsense. I shouldn't listen to the words that say that I'm righteous. I'm a sinner." I published a book called, *The Secret of the Forgiveness of Sin and Being Born Again*. And some people wrote some words against me saying, "I hereby declare myself a sinner until the day I die." This person is just like the minister of the king. The judgment of man is not correct. The Word of God is correct.

Even though we are sinners in our own eyes, we are righteous if God says we are justified. The more we read the Bible, the clearer it becomes that our sins have been washed away, and we have been made righteous through Jesus being crucified.

The 66 books of the Bible are filled with these kinds of words. In Isaiah chapter 44, verse 22 it says, *I have blotted out, as a thick cloud, thy transgressions, and, as a cloud, thy sins: return unto me; for I have redeemed thee. (Isaiah 44:22)* God says, "I have blotted out your sins and transgressions like a thick cloud. Return unto me." I used to live believing in my own thoughts, however, I began to believe the Word of God.

No matter what my thoughts are, if God says I am justified, then I believe that I am righteous. No matter how it looks in my eyes, if God says that my sins have been washed, then I believe my sins have been washed. Believing the Word of God is believing in God.

People who believe in their own thoughts believe in themselves. They cannot enjoy the grace and blessings of God. The man of God said to the minister of the king, "You will see it with your eyes, but you will not eat thereof." Because I told many lies and stole a lot, I clearly knew that I was a sinner. But when I read the Bible, the Bible did not say that. God did not say that. God said that my sins have been washed away by the blood of Jesus. Should I believe my own thoughts, or should I believe the Word of God? Who am I to believe in myself? I am not someone worthy to be believed in. That's why I began to believe the Word of God.

I have lied and stolen many, many times, but I believe that I am righteous. Believing the Word of God because it fits your heart and not believing because it doesn't…that's not truly believing in God—it is trusting yourself. No matter how it looks in your eyes, believing in the Word of God is what it means to believe God.

I used to live in despair in 1962, but I discovered that all my sins have been cleansed through reading the Bible. Before that, I always begged for my sins to be forgiven, but I did not beg after that. Why? I had been freely made righteous by the grace of God. God changed my life from then on. I could feel Him with me in all that I did. God worked amazingly when I believed in Him.

God Who Worked Through the Footsteps of the Four Lepers

Through God's work, the four lepers went to the Syrian camp near twilight, looking for food. God worked through them. As they stumbled and fell, God changed the sound of their footsteps into a terrible army, galloping horses, rumbling chariot wheels, and the roars of countless people.

God caused the Syrian soldiers to hear that. They were outside their tents, trying to make food and eat, when they heard those sounds. They were shocked when they came out of their tents. It was twilight, so they were unable to see anything. However, they heard tremendous sounds. They asked themselves, "What are these sounds?" Among them, a smart person said, "Surely, the king of Israel must have paid the Pharoah of Egypt and the kings of other countries so they could hire many soldiers. Now, they have arrived to attack us." Then the rest of the Syrian soldiers yelled, "Oh my, we better run!" They didn't even get on their horses. They just fled by foot.

Soon afterwards, the four lepers arrived at the Syrian camp and said, "We surrender. Do not kill us!" However, there were no signs of life. They searched the tents, and there was no one to be found. There was only abandoned food still boiling in pots. They thought to themselves, "Is this a dream, or is this reality?" They were so happy. Then they said, "Okay, let's eat first, and then take a look around. If we are going to die, then let's eat and die." And they mindlessly ate all they could. Because they were full, they hid the gold and silver they found in the tents. Then one of the lepers said, "We do not do well. Today is a day of good tidings, and we hold our peace. If we tarry until the morning light, some mischief will come upon us. Now, let us go and tell the city of Samaria there is a lot of food here."

The four lepers arrived at the city of Samaria. They cried out, "Hello! We went to the Syrian camp. We have seen that the tents and food are just lying everywhere. But there are no soldiers there!" That night, the people of Samaria went to the Syrian camp and brought the food back to the city. The next morning, one measure of fine flour was sold for a shekel, and two measures of barely for a shekel. The king's minister who was keeping the city gate was trampled by the people and died. Then, according to the words of the man of God, "You shall see it with your eyes, but shall not eat thereof," was achieved.

Let us not be like the king's minister, but people who believe in the Word of God. Whether my sins were washed away or not, let us not believe what arises in our thoughts, but in the words of the Bible. The Bible says that our sins have been washed perfectly by the blood of Jesus. God says that He does not remember our sins. I do not believe my thoughts—I believe in the words of God. From then on, God worked amazingly in me.

It is the person who believes the Word of God who is blessed. The person who believes that his sins have been washed as white as snow is a blessed person. The king's minister was unable to believe the Word of God, and he saw the tremendous amount of food, but couldn't eat it.

No matter what our thoughts are, if you accept that our sins have been washed by the blood of Jesus by faith, I believe the infinite grace and blessings of God will overflow in you.

Chapter 8

The Blind Man Who Went to the Pool of Siloam According to the Word

The Blind Man Who Went to the Pool of Siloam According to the Word

I am so thankful I can speak about the words of God together with all of you. All the words in the Bible are the precious promises God has given us. Satan tries to confuse people's hearts in order to lead their hearts in a different direction than the Word of God. However, God has recorded His word precisely in the Bible. And inside of the Bible, you can see the heart of God. Whoever accepts the Word of God will experience a new, amazing world.

The Gospel of John has particularly many writings that draw our hearts close to the heart of Jesus. But John chapter 9 is also teaching us something very important.

We will read from John chapter 9, verses 1 through 12:

And as Jesus passed by, he saw a man which was blind from his birth. And his disciples asked him, saying, Master, who did sin, this man, or his parents, that he was born blind? Jesus answered, Neither hath this man sinned, nor his parents: but that the works of God should be made manifest in him. I must work the works of him that sent me, while it is day: the night cometh, when no man can work. As long as I am in the world, I am the light of the world. When he had thus spoken, he spat on the ground, and made clay of the spittle, and he anointed the eyes of the blind man with the clay, And said unto him, Go, wash in the pool of Siloam, (which is by interpretation, Sent.) He went his way therefore, and washed, and came seeing. The neighbours therefore, and they which before had seen him that he was blind, said, Is not this he that sat and begged? Some said, This is he: others said, He is like him: but he said, I am he. Therefore said they unto him, How were thine eyes opened? He answered and said, A man that is called Jesus made clay, and anointed mine eyes, and said unto me, Go to the pool of Siloam, and wash: and I went and washed, and I received sight. Then said they unto him, Where is he? He said, I know not. (John 9:1-12)

The Bible, Which Has Illustrated the Process of How New Heart Is Formed in Us

The book of John talks to us about the change in

our hearts. A long time ago, people had to walk long distances. Then, cars were invented so that people could comfortably travel long distances. The Bible tells us about the process of how thoughts that are completely different than the ones we had before are made in our hearts.

For example, in John chapter 8 the story of the woman taken in the act of adultery appears. This woman committed adultery with a man, and she was being dragged out into the open to be stoned. Then she met Jesus. The Bible has simply recorded the events. However, within this record, you can clearly see this woman's heart.

Why did this woman commit adultery? It was a lustful heart that arose in her. However, if you take a closer look, you will see that this was not necessarily the case. Everyone experiences a lustful heart arise in them. Just because we have those hearts does not mean we all commit adultery. In addition to that, when you were caught committing adultery in the time of this woman, you were stoned to death. This woman knew what would happen if she were to be caught. So why would she do such a scary thing?

The thought that arose in her was, "If I do it without anybody knowing, then no one will find out. I will not get caught." She believed that thought. However, getting caught meant her stoning. Then, no matter what lustful heart arose in her, would she still be able to commit adultery? If she had the heart, "If I do this, I will not get caught," then she would believe in that thought and commit adultery. Ultimately, this woman believed her thoughts. When she committed adultery because she believed in her thoughts and was caught, she must have been so regretful and despaired. This woman was in a situation where she had to be stoned to death. People spat on her and kicked her. Through it all, she had no choice but to be dragged in this direction. She must have been so afraid, but soon afterwards, she met Jesus.

The Pharisees and scribes brought her to Jesus, and they asked Him, "Sir, this woman was caught in the act of adultery. Moses in the law commanded that such a woman should be stoned, but Master, what do you say?" Jesus wrote on the ground with His finger. Then He got up and He said, "He that is without sin among you, let him first cast the stone at her." Until that moment, people only saw her sin of committing adultery. They did not have the eyes to see their own sins. The words Jesus spoke allowed them to look inside of their own hearts. They, too, had dirty hearts inside. They were ashamed. Then they put down the stones that they had picked up to throw at the woman, one by one. And, one by one, they just went away.

Jesus saw this woman and said, "Woman, where are those thine accusers? Hath no one condemned thee?"

This woman looked around, and there was none there, so she replied, "No man, Lord."

Then Jesus said, "Neither do I condemn thee, go and sin no more."

I thought about this woman's heart. First, she had a lustful heart. She thought she wouldn't get caught if she did everything according to her thoughts. When she committed adultery and got caught, her heart was full of fear. She thought, "Is it all over for me? Those stones are going to fly at me, hit my head, and break my face. Then, I am going to bleed, and I will die."

Right then, she met Jesus, and He said, "Neither do I condemn thee, go and sin no more."

I thought about the image of this woman hearing the words of Jesus, and returning home. With a truly humble heart towards Jesus, she would have said, "Lord, thank you." As she returned home, her heart was filled with Jesus. "If it were not for Jesus, my head would have been hit by stones. My ribs would have been broken. I would have bled out and I should be dead. I should have been under a pile of stones by now. However, I am walking home alive. Jesus is the one who saved me. He also said that He does not condemn me." When she finally arrived at home, and opened the door, she thought to herself, "I thought I'd never be able to open these doors again. I thought that I was never going to be able to sleep in this bed again. Wow, Jesus saved my life."

This woman's heart changed into a whole new world after she met Jesus. It was now overflowing with thankfulness and gratitude. She would wake up several times while sleeping, thinking, "I'm not dreaming, am I? I am alive and back home, right? This is all because of Jesus. I'm so thankful, and so grateful. Lord, thank you." This woman's heart was full of thankfulness and joy. Her heart was so full of thankfulness, there was no room for anything else. There was no room for any dark thoughts to enter her heart. This woman lived with a thankful heart, praising God. Jesus also changes our hearts as amazingly as this.

The Blind Man Was Led to a Whole New World After Meeting Jesus

There is a blind man who appears in John chapter 9. This person was born blind and had never once seen the light. He lived thinking, "I heard that roses are pretty, but what does pretty look like? I heard that the sky above the mountains is blue, but what is blue?" He lived without understanding any of that. However, he would wake up in the morning, go out, and diligently beg for money because he needed to survive.

That was how he lived, and then one day, he met Jesus. The disciples of Jesus said, "I heard that this man was blind from birth. How much sin did he have that he was born blind? Wait. There's no way he could have sinned before he was born. How could he have committed sin inside the womb? His parents must have been the sinners. But if the parents sinned, then the parents should have been blind. Why did he become blind?"

The disciples could not discern whether this person was born blind because of himself or his parents. So, they asked Jesus, "Master, did this person become blind because of his own sins, or because of his parents' sins?"

Jesus answered, "It is not because of his sins or his parents' sins. This has happened so that the works of God should be manifest in him. I must do the work of Him that has sent me while it is day." Then he spat on the ground and made some clay. Jesus put the clay on the eyes of the blind man and said, "Go wash in the pool of Siloam."

I believe that the blind man thought, "This man is putting something on my eyes. Should I ask him for some money?" Begging and getting money, and the joy of eating food with that money was everything to this person's life. But after meeting Jesus, this blind man was able to have a new heart that he's never had before.

After Jesus put the clay on his eyes, He said, "Go, and wash in the pool of Siloam." The blind man never once thought to go to the pool of Siloam. Jesus instilled the heart of wanting to go to Siloam into the blind man. This was not a heart the blind man had on his own. However, the words of Jesus entered him and stirred up a new heart in him.

For us to live spiritual life well, it is not that we need to pray well or give a lot of offering. It is not that we need to be sincere with all our hearts, nor do we need to confess our sins. The most important thing is for us to receive the heart of Jesus that we never had before.

The blind man never once thought of going to the pool of Siloam. If the blind person tries to go to the pool, it's dangerous, and he could slip and fall in. He would never have thought of going to the pool of Siloam and wash there. In fact, the only thing he thought about was filling his belly with pieces of bread. He wanted to come outside that morning to beg. Even just a little while ago, he was begging for bread. However, he stopped doing that and went to the pool of Siloam.

Along the way, he asked people, "Excuse me, is

this the right way to the pool of Siloam? Are there any rough patches along the way? Any pits? Is there a steep incline on the way to Siloam?" The blind man had lived following his own thoughts until that moment. He was the same person, but now he was being led by a completely different world. He had lived his life trying to take care of his hunger. He lived trying to get more food—that was all that he lived for. He kept moving in order to get better bread. He lived following after the desires of his flesh of wanting to be comfortable.

However, after meeting Jesus, the desires of the flesh to take care of his hunger no longer led him. The words of Jesus were leading him. So many people in this world live after the desires of their flesh like this blind man. No matter what kind of a person you are, the desires of the flesh and your own wants are everything, before you meet Jesus. But just like the blind man, Jesus will lead your heart once you meet Him.

You can see the difference between the people who are led by the heart of Jesus, and the people who are led by the desires of the flesh. When the blind man went to the pool of Siloam, he did not go there just to get a few coins. The words of Jesus led him to the pool of Siloam.

What are you led by? Are you not being led by the desires of your flesh? Intead of being moved by desires, an idea of the future, and/or things that look good, if you are led by Jesus like the blind man, who allowed Jesus to lead his footsteps all the way to the pool of Siloam, you will not live your life the same way. You can never be the same person again once you get to live a new life through Jesus.

There are many people who go to church today, and they become deacons and elders. They give a lot of offering, read the bible, and pray, but they live according to their own thoughts. It is rare to find people who accept the words and heart of Jesus, and who live through Him. Even though you have lived according to the desires of your flesh until now, if you accept the words of Jesus and are led by Him, and you are no longer led by your flesh, you become the children of God. You become amazing, tremendous people.

October, 1962: When the Words of Jesus Entered My Heart

I went to church from a young age, but I was always led by the desires of the flesh. In October of 1962, the words of Jesus came into my heart and began to lead me. I heard that Jesus died on the cross for my sins many times, but I still believed I was a sinner. The true meaning of Jesus' crucifixion had not come upon my heart. I simply said that I was a sinner because I committed sins. I thought that was everything.

But one day, my thoughts changed. "Even though I committed sins, if Jesus carried my sins and died on the cross instead of me, then I am not a sinner. If Jesus shed His blood for me, my sins have been washed away." That was the heart that I had. It was amazing. From then on, the Bible looked different every time I read it, although it was the same Bible. I was shocked by this.

In the past, the only the parts of the Bible that entered

my heart were the verses that told me I was a sinner. But after receiving the forgiveness of sins, there were so many places in the Bible telling me my sins were washed. The Bible was telling me that I had been cleansed, that I was holy. The Bible also says that I'm justified, and that I'm honorable. My heart and my life, which used to be suffering and lost in sin, completely changed.

My sins have been washed away. It was an unbelievable truth, but I believed in it because it was in the Word of God. I am righteous, I am holy, even a dirty person like me. The more I thought about this, the more amazing it was. It is not that I did not sin—the blood of Jesus paid the entire price for the sins I've committed. God tells me that I am justified in many places throughout the Bible. He says that He does not condemn me. He says that my sins are washed away, forever. In the past, I questioned, "Why did I read the Bible? Why did I say that I was a sinner? Why was I so worried because of sin?" My life completely changed.

The blind man who heard the words of Jesus and washed his face and eyes in the pool of Siloam, had his eyes opened. When we look to see what he did afterwards, we find that he testifies of Jesus. He became very busy testifying that Jesus was the Son of God.

Decades ago, there were no luxury cars in our country. So, people drove cars that were uncomfortable. Cars, nowadays, are really good and really powerful. But a long time ago, Korea's technological capabilities to build engines were far inferior to what they are now. After you drove a car for a certain number of miles, the pistons would wear out. So, when the pistons compressed air into the cylinders, the air would leak out on the side and reduce the power to the engine. To resolve that, the engine had to be rebuilt. Cars today are built really well, so they rarely become undriveable because of a bad engine. Even if you drive a car for 200,000 kilometers, the engine will not have any problems.

Our lives can also be renewed the same way cars become improved. In Gangnam, Seoul, there are many plastic surgery clinics where you can undergo cosmetic procedures. You can make your eyes look bigger. You can reduce your cheekbones. You can also get a nose job. So people get their faces worked on, here and there. A lot of people visit from overseas to get their faces done.

After some college students graduate, they comment on how much their faces have changed when they meet up after a long while apart. "Hey, where did you get your nose done? Where did you get your double eyelids done?" These cosmetic surgery clinics change a person's physical images, but Jesus changes our hearts. The same way you remove a broken car engine and install a new one, you will experience amazing change—to be like Jesus—when you throw away your heart, which is not good, and accept the heart of Jesus.

Jesus Who Changed My Heart Also Healed My Heart

After I believed in the Word of God, it was so amazing to see how God worked in my life. In 1999, my heart was very ill. While I was in the army, I received ranger training, which was very difficult. And the pre-ranger training exercises you had to do were also very difficult. During ranger training, you have to slide down a cable wire from the top of a mountain. As part of the training, you had to slide down the cable and let go and fall into the river. When you are coming down on the wire, it's very important to get the timing right when you let go. If you let go too early, or too late, you could land in a very shallow section of the river, or you could land completely outside of the river and get badly injured.

Those are the times when you should not look to your own judgement. You should look at the trainer. When the trainer raises the flag, you have to let go of the cable, and fall away. That's when you will land safely in the deeper water. There are also lots of other dangers when it comes to different aspects of the training. Accidents can happen when you lose focus, so we all had to complete very difficult and intense physical training beforehand in order to increase our focus.

One time we were told to assemble, so I ran to the assembly line. However, my body would not listen, so, I collapsed and could not stand up. That's when I discovered for the first time that my heart was unhealthy. I took about three days off. Back then, I was young, so I became well again. However, after I passed the age of 50, it began to be more and more obvious that my heart was ill. When I put a stethoscope on my heart and listened to my heart, my heart would be beat, beat, beat, and then stop. I felt this weird sensation. I got nervous because my heart would stop beating and stay still. Fortunately, it would start beating again a few seconds later.

When I turned 50 years old, I thought that I wasn't going to live past the age of 60. In 1999, when I was 55 years old, my heart was in very bad condition. I thought to myself, "Will I even have another month to live?" At that moment, we were building our mission center. When I looked up from the ground level to the people working on the 7th floor, my heart was pounding, and it felt like it was going to stop. So, I closed my eyes.

The summer of that year, we had a summer retreat at the Sungho Pine Field. One night, as I was laying down to sleep, I thought about what happened during the day. The distance from the main office area of the retreat to the Sunday school section was about 500 meters. I made four round trips that day, which means I walked about 4 km. With my heart like that, that was something that could not be done. I had the heart that God healed me. I woke up the next morning, and I jogged around the farms surrounding the pine fields. From then on, I went jogging every morning.

Even after the retreat was over, I would go jogging early every morning at the West Daejeon Girl's High School, which was near my church. The track at that school was 300 meters. In the beginning, after two laps, I would be so out of breath and unable to run anymore. But as I ran every day, the distance I could run gradually increased. It went from 1 km to 2 km. Then, 3 km, then 4 km. When I took a shower after sweating, my body felt so refreshed. I bought a pair of sneakers and carried them in my bag. I jogged early every morning when I traveled abroad. I ran in different countries throughout Africa, and I jogged in the streets of Saint Petersburg, Russia. My heart condition improved so much. There are too many works that God did in my life for me to talk about them all.

Now the Heart of Jesus Led the Blind Man

In John chapter 9, the blind man started the day with his own heart. When the day began, he had his breakfast, went out to the street, and stretched out his hands to beg. That was how he lived his daily life trying to get bread to fulfill the desires of his flesh.

Then one day, he met Jesus. After Jesus spat on the ground and made some clay, He applied it on the blind man's eyes. Then He told him, "Go wash in the pool of Siloam." When he heard the words of Jesus, the blind man went to the pool of Siloam. This was not the thought of the blind man. The will of Jesus led him to the pool of Siloam.

The blind man lived his entire life according to his own thoughts. However, after hearing the words of Jesus, those words entered his heart, and he began to be led by those thoughts. In the past, the desires of his flesh strung him along. Now, however, the heart of Jesus was leading him. He asked everyone he came across, "Excuse me, I need to go to Siloam. Is this the right way to go? How much longer do I have to go? Are there any pits or deep ditches along the way? I'm sorry to keep asking, but I'm blind. Thank you so much for kindly guiding me."

The blind man asked around and found his way to the pool of Siloam. He finally arrived at the pool. He asked, "This is the pool of Siloam, right?"

Someone answered, "Yes, it is."

He cautiously tried to feel his way around the pool of Siloam with his hands. If the blind man fell into the water, he would not know which way to get out—it was very dangerous for him. Carefully, he went down, step by step, and his hands finally touched the waters. He scooped up water with his hands and washed his face. He washed his face for a good while, and his eyes began to feel numb. Then he began to see something. "What's this? It's moving. Oh, this is my face! This is what I look like." For the first time in his life, he saw his face reflected in the water. He looked at the bright, shining sun and thought, "That's the sun that everybody was talking about."

The words of Jesus entered the blind man and led him. The heart of Jesus is in the Word of God. When the heart of Jesus entered the blind man, he started to change. His eyes were opened, and he saw the world for the first time. "Ah, this is how I look. This is what people look like. What does my mother look like? I want to quickly go and see." A heart he did not have before sprang up inside of him. Now, he didn't have to ask other people for directions anymore. He walked back on his own.

There is something interesting in these scriptures. From verse 8, when the blind man returned healed, the neighbors and the people who had seen him be before, asked about this to each other.

"Isn't he the one who used sit and beg?"

Some said it is he, and some said that it is someone like him. When the blind man said, "I am he," the people started to ask, "How were your eyes opened?"

"A man named Jesus made clay and put it on my eyes, and told me to wash in Siloam. I did, and I am able to see."

From that moment on, people began to speak badly of Jesus. That day was a Sabbath Day, but Jesus didn't keep the Sabbath Day. Because He worked, they said He was not a person from God. However, what they all said did not enter into the heart of the blind man because Jesus' heart had already filled it up.

Spiritual life is not about, thinking, "I better pray well. I better witness well. I better do good deeds." It is about accepting the Word of God. The words of the Bible are all the words of God. They are the words of Jesus. The heart of Jesus is in the words of the Bible. That's why the heart of Jesus enters us when we accept His word. That's also why we should not argue about this and that when the Word of God in front of us. If they are words from the Bible, we need to simply accept them into our hearts.

The People Who Push the Word of God Away

The words that changed my life were in Romans chapter 3, verse 24. In Romans chapter 3, verse 23, it says, *For all have sinned, and come short of the glory of God.* But in verse 24, it says, *Being justified freely by his grace through the redemption that is in Christ Jesus.* God tells us that we are justified. If we accept these words into our hearts exactly as they are, we can say, "Even though I committed sins, if God says I am justified, then I am righteous." If God says that we're justified, then we're righteous. If God says we're sanctified, then we're holy. If He says that we're graced, then we are graced. However, people do not think so. Even though God clearly says that we're justified in the Bible, people think on their own and come to this conclusion, "Am I righteous? No, I'm not righteous. I have many sins. I'm a sinner."

If we are still sinners, but God sees us and says we are righteous, then God is a liar. God calls us righteous because we are righteous. God could never call a sinner righteous. If God could call a sinner righteous, then there would be no need for Jesus to die on the cross. God could just call people righteous. However, because God could never call a sinner righteous, Jesus had to be crucified and die on the cross. Jesus needed to wash all of our sins through the blood shed on the cross. Because we became righteous through the redemption of Jesus, God says that we are righteous. When the blood that Jesus shed on the cross appears unclear, and you clearly remember the sins you've committed, that's when you call yourself a sinner.

On the other hand, people who clearly know that the blood Jesus Christ shed on the cross washed away all of our sins can never say that they are sinners. We cannot say that we're sinners without denying that Jesus washed away all of our sins. God tells us that we are justified. He says that we are sanctified. He says that He remembers our sins no more.

Saying that you are a sinner is not a humble thing to do. Denying that you have been forgiven by the blood of Jesus is going against God. I wrote in the book, *The Secret of the Forgiveness of Sin and Being Born Again,* that my sins have been washed away and I have been made righteous. One pastor mentioned my book and said, "I hereby declare that I am a sinner until the day I die." It is complete nonsense. If you're a sinner until the day you die, then what happened to the cross? Does it mean that the cross of Jesus did not wash away our sins? Is he saying that Jesus died in vain?

Spiritual Life Is Having the Heart of Jesus Inside of You

Before I got saved, I only had my own thoughts in my heart. However, as the word entered my heart, I could feel that it was no longer my thoughts but the Word of God that was leading me. The thoughts of the blind man led him until he met Jesus in John chapter 9.

After meeting Jesus, the words of Jesus entered his heart. Jesus said, "Go, wash in the pool of Siloam." The blind man went and washed in the pool of Siloam according to Jesus' words. His eyes were opened. He met people, and he told them that Jesus opened his eyes. Amazing things that he had never thought of before began to happen in his life. In my heart, I imagined this person getting a job, meeting a beautiful woman, getting married, having sons and daughters, and living happily.

The woman taken in the act of adultery was supposed to be stoned to death, but she met Jesus. The words of Jesus entered her heart: "Neither do I condemn thee, go and sin no more." New thoughts arose in this woman's heart. "Ah, I am not condemned. My sins are forgiven. I am thankful." Believing in Jesus is not praying hard, giving lots of offering, helping others, or doing good deeds. It's about having a heart that is different from your own. It's having the heart of Jesus. However, people are unable to do that. They think of themselves as sinners since they committed sins.

Jesus washed away all of our sins, and we have been made clean and righteous. That's why the Bible says that we are righteous. However, people do not accept the word, and so, they have their own thoughts and call themselves sinners. That is a person who believes in his or her own thoughts. That is not a person who believes in Jesus. That person has nothing to do with the blood of Jesus, and Jesus cannot work in that person.

When you read the Bible, you have to accept whatever the word into your heart. Even though you may see something as dirty and evil with your eyes, if the Bible says you're justified, it means that you're righteous. If the Bible says that you're sanctified, you're holy. Your thought are one thing, the Bible is another. If your thoughts win, you will say, "That's right, I'm a sinner. I committed sins, so how could I say I have no sins? It's nonsense." But if the Word of God wins, then you will say, "I committed many sins, but God says that I am righteous. He says that my sins have been washed as white as snow. He says that He remembers my sins no more. Therefore, I am righteous."

Even though I went to church, I met many people who said that they are sinners. The people who say that they are sinners do so because they do not accept the Word of God that says that we are righteous. In the Bible, there are so many words that tell us that we have been justified. *Who was delivered for our offences, and was raised again for our justification. (Romans 4:25)*

Jesus died to wash away our sins, and He rose again for our justification. After receiving the punishment for all of our sins, he came back to life and told us, "I received all the punishment for every one of your sins. Therefore, you are righteous." But people say, "No, I'm a sinner." That is going against Jesus. Many people go to church today and call themselves sinners. When the Word of God enters our hearts and overcomes our thoughts, we become people of God. We, too, become righteous, just like God said. However, the thoughts that come from having a conscience overpowers the word. People can't fathom proclaiming their righteousness after committing so many sins—countless people are still caught under this heart.

When we look at 1 Corinthians chapter 6, verse 10, there are amazing words there. *Nor thieves, nor covetous, nor drunkards, nor revilers, nor extortioners, shall inherit the kingdom of God. (1 Corinthians 6:10)* The people who do commit these sins cannot inherit the kingdom of heaven. However, 1 Corinthians chapter 6, verse 11 says, *And such were some of you...* This means that we all have stolen, we all have coveted, we all were drunken, we all have reviled, and we all have extorted. However, after this, verse 11 continues with, ...*but ye are washed, but ye are sanctified, but ye are justified in the name of the Lord Jesus, and by the Spirit of our God.*

The expression here is really good. You have committed these sins, but you are washed. But you are sanctified. But you are justified. Will you believe your own thoughts, or will you believe the Word of God? God speaks the word to us, "You have committed sins, but you are washed, but you are sanctified, but you are justified." When you believe these words, you can say, "I am righteous."

I was a sinner until I was 18 years old. In 1962, I realized that my sins had been washed clean. No matter how much I thought about it, I was righteous. Even though I committed many sins, Jesus washed them all away at the cross, so I was righteous, no matter what anybody said. I threw away my thoughts that told me I was a sinner—I accepted the Word of God by faith.

After the woman taken in the act of adultery met Jesus, her life was saved. She returned home, and as she was sleeping, she must have had unspeakable thankfulness in her heart. "If it wasn't for Jesus, my head and my back would have been broken, and I would be dead. Right now, I should be under a pile of stones. But Jesus saved my life." I also had my own day. "My sins have been washed away. By the blood of Jesus, my sins have been washed as white as snow. Now I am not a sinner." The more I thought about it, the more amazed and thankful I was. From that day on, until this day, I continue to testify this truth.

For By One Offering, He Hath Perfected Forever Them That Are Sanctified

In the Bible, there are many words about how our sins have been forgiven. Hebrews chapter 10 especially writes about this in great detail. *By the which will we are sanctified through the offering of the body of Jesus Christ once for all. (Hebrews 10:10)* Here, it says that our sins have been washed through Jesus offering up His body and dying on the cross. And thus, we are sanctified.

And every priest standeth daily ministering and offering oftentimes the same sacrifices, which can never take away sins. (Hebrews 10:11) The priests of the Old Testament continued to kill goats and lambs to give sin offerings. Those offerings were able to wash away sins that were committed. But if a person sins again, then they become sinners again. Therefore, those offerings could not take away sins for all time.

This world belongs to the realm of time. We have the past, the present, and the future. Time continues to pass. For example, suppose a person steals something and gives a sin offering to wash away the sin—that offering will flow into the past. If that person commits another sin, the past sin offering is no longer effective. Therefore, another lamb needs to be killed and given as an offering. Because offerings need to be given every time they sin, it says that blood flowed like a river underneath the sin altar, and the smoke that rose from the burning of the sin offerings were like clouds during Old Testament times. The offering that Jesus gave on this earth was different from the offerings given in the Old Testament. Jesus did not give the offering on the altar on earth. He presented His offering at the temple in heaven.

Hebrews chapter 9, verse 11 tells us about that: *By the which will we are sanctified through the offering of the body of Jesus Christ once for all. (Hebrews 9:11)* The greater and more perfect tabernacle not made with hands represents the temple in heaven. The temple is in heaven, and Moses saw that temple and replicated it as the tabernacle on earth, a structure made by the hands of man.

Afterwards, the temple on earth was built in the time of King Solomon. What is the difference between heaven and earth? Everything on earth changes. Gold changes, and silver changes. But in heaven, nothing changes. Because it's an eternal world, it should not change. No matter how strong our body is, it ages, more and more, and ultimately, it dies. In heaven, things do not change, and therefore, it's eternal. It is an eternal life there, and thus, the washing away of our sins is also eternal. Jesus did not sprinkle His blood at the altar on earth. He sprinkled His blood on the altar in heaven.

Neither by the blood of goats and calves, but by his own blood he entered in once into the holy place, having obtained eternal redemption for us. (Hebrews 9:12) He obtained eternal redemption for every person through the blood that Jesus shed on the cross, sprinkled on the altar in eternal heaven. The sin offering does not need to be given many times because our sins have been washed away forever.

It was finished once and for all. *By the which will we are sanctified through the offering of the body of Jesus*

Christ once for all. (Hebrews 10:10) On earth, you had to give a sin offering every time a sin was committed. In heaven, the sin has been washed away forever, so we are righteous forever. God has made us righteous and holy forever. These words are the words of God. They are different from our thoughts. Our thoughts change every day. Do not believe them. Believe the Word of God, which never changes. The offerings given in the Old Testament are a shadow that portrays the eternal sacrifice that would be given by Jesus Christ.

In Hebrews chapter 10, verses 11 through 13 say, *And every priest standeth daily ministering and offering oftentimes the same sacrifices, which can never take away sins: But this man, after he had offered one sacrifice for sins for ever, sat down on the right hand of God; From henceforth expecting till his enemies be made his footstool. (Hebrews 10:11-13)* Jesus gave the eternal offering. Now, let's take a look at verse 14: *For by one offering he hath perfected for ever them that are sanctified. (Hebrews 10:14)* Jesus perfected us forever because He has washed our sins away forever.

Whereof the Holy Ghost also is a witness to us: for after that he had said before, this is the covenant that I will make with them after those days, saith the Lord, I will put my laws into their hearts, and in their minds will I write them; And their sins and iniquities will I remember no more. Now where remission of these is, there is no more offering for sin. (Hebrews 10:15-18)

Jesus has washed away our sins forever—that means there are no more offerings to be given. This is the fact that we believe. And we are so thankful for it. Jesus has washed us perfectly clean. You are holy, and you are righteous. Do not be deceived by Satan. Do not trust your thoughts. I hope you will believe these words, and then I believe the unspeakable blessings of God will be added unto you.

Chapter 9

At the Crossroads of Works and Grace

At the Crossroads of Works and Grace

God is making a new world of the heart inside of us that we have never known before. After we receive this heart, we get to see how great the heart God gives us really is. We'll read from Genesis chapter 27, verse 1 through 40:

> And it came to pass, that when Isaac was old, and his eyes were dim, so that he could not see, he called Esau his eldest son, and said unto him, My son: and he said unto him, Behold, here am I. And he said, Behold now, I am old, I know not the day of my death: Now therefore take, I pray thee, thy weapons, thy quiver and thy bow, and go out to the field, and take me some venison; And

*make me savoury meat, such as I love, and bring it to
me, that I may eat; that my soul may bless thee before
I die. And Rebekah heard when Isaac spake to Esau
his son. And Esau went to the field to hunt for venison,
and to bring it. And Rebekah spake unto Jacob her
son, saying, Behold, I heard thy father speak unto Esau
thy brother, saying, Bring me venison, and me savoury
meat, that I may eat, and bless thee before the Lord
before my death. Now therefore, my son, obey my voice
according to that which I command thee. Go now to
the flock, and fetch me from thence two good kids of
the goats; and I will make them savoury meat for thy
father, such as he loveth: And thou shalt bring it to
thy father, that he may eat, and that he may bless thee
before his death. And Jacob said to Rebekah his mother,
Behold, Esau my brother is a hairy man, and I am a
smooth man: My father peradventure will feel me, and
I shall seem to him as a deceiver; and I shall bring a
curse upon me, and not a blessing. And his mother said
unto him, Upon me be thy curse, my son: only obey my
voice, and go fetch me them. And he went, and fetched,
and brought them to his mother: and his mother made
savoury meat, such as his father loved. And Rebekah
took goodly raiment of her eldest son Esau, which were
with her in the house, and put them upon Jacob her
younger son: And she put the skins of the kids of the
goats upon his hands, and upon the smooth of his neck:
And she gave the savoury meat and the bead, which
she had prepared, unto the hand of her son Jacob. And
he came to his father, and said, My father: and he*

said, Here am I, who art thou, my son? And Jacob said unto his father, I am Esau thy firstborn; I have done according as thou badest me: arise, I pray thee, sit and eat of my venison, that thy soul may bless me. And Isaac said unto his son, How is it that thou hast found it so quickly, my son? And he said, Because the Lord thy God brought it to me. And Isaac said unto Jacob, Come near, I pray thee, that I may feel thee, my son, whether thou be my very son Esau or not. And Jacob went near unto Isaac his father; and he felt him, and said, The voice is Jacob's voice, but the hands are the hands of Esau. And he discerned him not, because his hands were hairy, as his brother Esau's hands: so he blessed him. And he said, Art thou my very son Esau? And he said, I am. And he said, Bring it near to me, and I will eat of my of my son's venison, that my soul may bless thee. And he brought it near to him, and he did eat: and he brought him wine, and he drank. And his father Isaac said unto him, Come near now, and kiss me, my son. And he came near, and kissed him: and he smelled the smell of his raiment, and blessed him, and said, See, the smell of my son is as the smell of a field which the Lord hath blessed: Therefore God give thee of the dew of heaven, and the fatness of the earth, and plenty of corn and wine: Let people serve thee, and nations bow down to thee: be lord over thy brethren, and let thy mother's sons bow down to thee: cursed be every one that curseth thee, and blessed be he that blesseth thee. And it came tot pass, as soon as Isaac had made an end of blessing Jacob, and Jacob was yet scarce gone out from the presence of Isaac his father, that Esau his brother came in from his hunting. And he also made savoury meat, and brought it unto his father, and said unto his father, Let my father arise, and eat of his son's venison, that thy soul may bless me. And Isaac his father said unto him, Who art thou? And he said, I am thy son, thy firstborn Esau. And Isaac trembled very exceedingly, and said, Who? where is he that hath taken venison, and brought it me, and I have eaten of all before thou camest, and have blessed him? yea, and he shall be blessed. And when Esau heard the words of his father, he cried with a great and exceeding bitter cry, and said unto his father, Bless me, even me also, O my father. And he said, Thy brother came with subtilty, and hath taken away thy blessing. And he said, Is not he rightly named Jacob? for he hath supplanted me these two times: he took away my birthright; and, behold, now he hath taken away my blessing. And he said, Hast thou not reserved a blessing for me? And Isaac answered and said unto Esau, Behold, I have made him thy lord, and all his brethren have I given to him for servants; and with corn and wine have I sustained him: and what shall I do now unto thee, my son? And Esau said unto his father, Hast thou but one blessing, my father? bless me, even me also, O my father. And Esau lifted up his voice, and wept. And Isaac his father answered and said unto him, Behold, thy dwelling shall be the fatness of the earth, and of the dew of heaven from above; And by thy sword shalt thou live, and shalt serve thy brother; and it shall come to pass when thou

shalt have the dominion, that thou shalt break his yoke
from off thy neck. (Genesis 27:1-40)

People Who Misunderstand What the Bible Is Meaning

We may read the Bible, but if we do not know the heart of God very well, we may understand it very differently. If we know the heart God wants to relay to us, then, we can easily understand what the Bible is saying. The Word of God is different from our thoughts. One of them is that we feel that we need to work hard, labor, and try hard to make sacrifices to be blessed by God. However, God teaches us that we cannot be blessed through that. Isaac wanted to give Esau the blessings. However, in the end, Esau could not be blessed. Jacob was blessed.

There's something God wants to teach us with this story. We must throw away all of our humanly thinking, and we must know the heart of God in order to receive the forgiveness of sins and be blessed. If we do not know the heart of God, then we cannot live a proper spiritual life.

Even when a husband and wife are living together, they must become one in heart. Parents and their children must be of one heart. Furthermore, we must also become one in heart with God. God wants to make our hearts well with Him, and He has expressed much of His heart in the Bible. The very sad thing is that even though we read the Bible, we understand the word through our own thoughts.

The story in Genesis chapter 27 is teaching us something very important: a person does not need to be honest, sincere, or truthful to be blessed by God. Unfortunately, those who do not know the heart of God contained in the Bible think that they have to be honest. They think that they need to work hard for God, and that they need to make a lot of effort. However, God is explaining that this is not true through Genesis chapter 27.

Many have read Genesis chapter 27 but are still unable to understand it because Esau hunted very sincerely as ordered by his father. Jacob lied, but then Jacob was blessed. As a result, there are many pastors who say that Jacob went through a lot of suffering and hardships because he lied and stole his older brother's blessings. This is the only explanation they could give because they did not know about the will of God,.

Salvation Received Only by Grace, Having Nothing to Do with Works

The Bible tells us very clearly about these things. However, since people have fallen into their own thoughts, for the most part, they don't know the heart of God very well. One of the stories in the Bible that people misunderstand is the story of the man who fell among thieves in Luke chapter 10. There are two kinds of people in the story—the savior and the saved.

In Luke chapter 10, a certain lawyer speaks to Jesus. He begins by asking Jesus a question, "What good must I do to inherit eternal life?" We don't obtain eternal life by doing something good. It has nothing to do with our works. It is by grace.

Ephesians chapter 2 tells us this: *For by grace are ye saved through faith; and that not of yourselves: it is the gift of God: Not by works, lest any man should boast. (Ephesians 2:8-9)* The Bible tells us that we receive salvation through grace, by faith. However, people think that they get saved through their hard work, diligence, and labor. That's why God needed people to realize that they don't receive salvation or are blessed through effort and hard work. So many people today think that they have to do good works for them to be saved. They think that they have to pray a lot, give a lot of offering, be diligent, and work hard. That is not true. None of those things are required to receive the forgiveness of sins and become born again. Look at the Bible. It is not through efforts.

For by grace are ye saved through faith; and that not of yourselves: it is the gift of God. (Ephesians 2:8) Grace cannot include even a small amount of effort. Paying for something is not grace. Grace is gaining something without doing anything for it. However, how many Christians in this world actually think that they can receive the grace of God without doing anything? Most people think that they have to keep the law, pray, and work hard.

The Reason God Gave the Tabernacle as He Gave the Commandments

In the story of the man who fell among thieves, you have the good Samaritan and the man who fell among thieves. One is a savior, while the other is the one who is saved. The man who fell among thieves was dying, and it was the good Samaritan who saved him. In this story, the man who fell among thieves represents us, who are dying of sin. So, who does the good Samaritan represent? He represents Jesus Christ. After Jesus was done with the parable, He told the lawyer to go and do the same.

God did not give us the law for us to try and keep it in order to be blessed. Of course, if you keep all of the laws, you will be blessed. However, God knew that man would not be capable of keeping the law. Therefore, when God gave the people of Israel the two tablets of stone containing the Ten Commandments through Moses, God didn't just give him the tablets of stone. Moses didn't just come down the mountain with the two tablets of stone— God showed him the temple in heaven. God showed him the sin altar, the water laver, lamp stand, the shewbread table, the incense altar, and the ark of the covenant. Then God said, "When you get down from this mountain, build the temple exactly as I've shown you." Why must the temple be made? Because the temple is where the sin offering is given to wash away sins. When the children of Israel committed sins, God gave them the temple to visit and give their offerings.

When the children of Israel said that they would keep all of the laws, did God believe them? God did not believe that man would do good and not commit sins. Therefore, when He gave them the law, they broke the law. And so, He also gave them the temple where they could have their sins washed away. If man does good deeds and does not commit sins, would there be a need for God to send Jesus Christ to this world? If you could live diligently, without committing sins, then why would you need Jesus? Yes, we committed sins and we did evil things, but more importantly, our sins can be washed away with no effort from us. Even the tiniest bit of our sins cannot be washed away through our efforts.

People were arrogant, people thought they could keep the law if they tried. Even though they broke the law, they continued to think, "If I do well from now on, I could be good." However, that is not true. In addition, we do not become righteous and holy by doing good.

There has never been anyone who could keep the law well enough to go to heaven. Every person has broken the law, and every person has to be cursed. In Luke chapter 10, a certain lawyer asks, "Jesus, what must I do to inherit eternal life?" Well, what must we do to inherit eternal life? If we pray, can we get eternal life? If we keep the law, or do good, can we get eternal life? Is eternal life attainable if we repent? None of these actions will work. We cannot receive eternal life by doing something. We cannot even wash away the tiniest sin by trying to do something. Why would Jesus be necessary if we could take care of our sins and attain eternal life that way? Jesus was crucified because nothing could be done with our own strength.

Why Was Jacob, Who Lied, Blessed?

Many people read Genesis chapter 27, but cannot comprehend it. Jacob lied, but he got blessed. People think, "Jacob lied, so why is God blessing him? Esau was honest, and he hunted and prepared the venison with all his heart, and then he brought it to his father like he was told. But Esau was cursed, and Jacob was blessed." For the most part, people do not understand what happened in Genesis chapter 27. Why was Jacob blessed even though he lied? And why did Esau act so diligently, but ended up a cursed man? The Bible tells us a very simple answer.

For by grace are ye saved through faith; and that not of yourselves: it is the gift of God. (Ephesians 2:8) How is salvation received? It is by grace, through faith. When it comes to grace, there is no wage. You cannot pay for it through your efforts or hard work. You simply receive it, freely. That's what grace is. Mankind has been deceived by Satan for a long time. Man has become used to wages. Students get an award as their wage for studying hard. People get paid for their hard work—that's a wage, too. We have grown accustomed to getting wages for what we've done.

God washing away our sins is not a wage. It is grace. God simply gives it to us, without any work on our part. God is so great and amazing that He didn't want to give something based on works. He wanted to bestow His grace on us.

When a baby is born, the mother breastfeeds the baby. Is that a wage or grace? It is grace. What could the baby do to earn a breastfeeding? A newborn baby will urinate, defecate, and continuously create problems. Then what wage could an infant receive? The mother does not give the child things based on a law of wages. A mother, as well as God, gives everything by grace. However, the lawyer asks Jesus, "What must I do to inherit eternal life?"

I met a famous pastor in a country I visited once. This pastor was sentenced to prison for 14 years for believing in God and suffered greatly as a result. I asked him, "Have you received the forgiveness of sins?" And then I asked him if he could go to heaven.

"I was in prison for 14 years for Jesus. Of course, I can go to heaven. Don't you think I could to go to heaven?"

I replied, "But the Bible does not say that. Heaven is not a place you get to go to by works. It is grace. Pastor, you going to prison is works."

Then he asked me, "Pastor, have you ever been to prison?"

"No, I have not. I've been to prisons to hold Bible studies, but I've never gone to jail for believing in Jesus."

"Pastor, do you think I was the only one who suffered when I went to prison? My kids had to eat fruit peels from the street. And my wife was persecuted. Do you know how great that pain was? And you're telling me I can't go to heaven?"

I answered him, "We cannot go to heaven through our works. Heaven is not a place where we can go to by our effort or labor."

The Lawyer Who Wrongly Thought That You Have to Do Something to Receive Eternal Life

In our lives, most of the things we've received have been wages for what we did. Salaries, awards, even compliments are wages. We have become so accustomed to living that way, so we think we have to try hard and receive the forgiveness of sins and the right to go to heaven as wages.

So, the lawyer came before Jesus and said, "What must I do to inherit, eternal life?"

Then Jesus asked the lawyer right back, "What is written in the law? And how readest thou?"

The lawyer replied, "The law says to love the Lord your God with all your heart, all your mind, all your strength, and all thy soul. And, you must love your neighbor as you love yourself." If you keep all the laws and do every one, then you can be blessed with eternal life. However, no one can do that.

I always want to read the Bible, so much so that I try to open my Bible when I hit red lights on the road while driving. I would read the Bible and fall into it. Then I would hear the car behind me honking their horn. The light had already turned green and every car in front of me had already passed. My car was the only one standing at the intersection. After that happened twice or so, I was afraid an accident might happen, so I was no longer able to read the Bible while waiting for the traffic light to turn green. If I poured my heart into reading the Bible while driving, I would not be able to drive the right way.

The point is, how could we possibly love God with all our hearts? If we were capable of doing that, we would not be able to have jobs. With all our heart, with all our soul, with all our strength, and with all our mind? We are unable to do that. It's impossible.

Jesus asked the lawyer, "What is written in the law, and how do you read it?" This means that the law can be read one way or another. How can we read the law then? We can read the law thinking, "If I try hard to keep the law, I can be blessed." On the other hand, we can read the law, thinking, "There's no way I can do this."

The lawyer, read the law saying, "You have to love the Lord, your God, with all your heart, all your soul, all your strength, and all your might. And you must love your neighbor as yourself."

Then Jesus told him, "If you do that, you can receive eternal life."

Right then, with the attitude that he could keep the law, the lawyer asked Jesus, "Then who is my neighbor?" Right then, Jesus told him the story about a man who fell among thieves.

We Must Become the Man Who Fell Among Thieves to Receive Salvation

There's a certain person who went down from Jerusalem to Jericho and fell among thieves. The thieves stripped him, beat him, and left him half dead. A priest was passing by that way but quickly crossed over to the other side. Then a Levite did the same thing. Afterwards, a good Samaritan was passing by and saved him. Jesus, spoke to the lawyer up until that point and said, "In your opinion, who of these three was neighbor to the man who fell among thieves?"

The lawyer answered, "The one who showed mercy on

him."

Jesus said, "Go, and do thou likewise."

Why did Jesus tell the lawyer, "Go, and do thou likewise?" The lawyer thought that he could do good. However, when you actually try to do this, you will realize that you are not able to do it. There were thieves all around. But, to treat the man who fell among thieves, to set him on your beast, to take him to an inn, to pay the necessary money to stay at the inn, and to offer to pay back whatever is spent later is not something one can do.

The priest saw the man who fell among the thieves and ran away. Why did he do that? He must have thought to himself, "This man fell among thieves. That must mean there's thieves around here. That means, I may also run into them. The same thing could happen to me." He could not help but run away at the thought of being hit by robbers, too. The Levite was the same way.

This good Samaritan did not regard the potential danger of saving this man. Instead, he saved the life of the man who fell among the thieves. This good Samaritan represents Jesus. Jesus gave His life for us. Jesus told the lawyer, "Go and do thou likewise. If you try do it, you will come to know that you are unable."

People who have not done it try to be like the good Samaritan. But if a person actually tries to do it, they come to realize that they're absolutely incapable. Who would risk their own life for the man who fell among thieves? The only one who can do that is Jesus Christ, alone. However, people deceive themselves, thinking, "I can still do it if I try." I want to ask you, "Can you love your neighbor as you love yourself? How could you love somebody else as much as you love yourself?" You cannot. This is not something you can do. Only Jesus can do it. It is not that we need to become the good Samaritan. We must become the man who fell among thieves, who receives salvation. However, many people today try hard to become the good Samaritan. Spiritual life becomes very exhausting with this approach. How could you give your life for others? It's very painful because you try to do something, but you end up incapable of actually doing it. Every individual who tries is deceived. It's just that they're trying hard to make themselves appear as if they're great.

What did the man who fell among thieves do to be saved? Did he save somebody else? He was in a position where he could only die. How could he do anything? People are fooled into thinking that they are the good Samaritan. They are fooled into thinking that if they try to do good, they can do good. They are fooled into thinking that if they try to keep the law, they can keep the law. They're fooled into thinking that they are good and kind people. They think of themselves as people who could help others.

You know, people like to act like they're great, holy, good, and sincere. This is all a lie. God has already said in the word that there is no good in man. There's only filthiness. Mankind is not the good Samaritan—mankind is the man who fell among thieves, the one who is dying. It's not that we need to do something as the man who fell among thieves. We should do nothing at all. The

Bible has expressed this so precisely, but we interpret it however we want. We are taught to do good, to try hard. And we think that only then, can we go to heaven.

For by grace are ye saved through faith; and that not of yourselves: it is the gift of God. (Ephesians 2:8) Salvation is not of us. It is the gift of God. It means that we should not try to receive salvation. It simply cannot happen through our efforts. It cannot happen through our good deeds. For us to be saved, Jesus must be the only one who works.

Countless people today hear the words of Jesus the wrong way, and so they inevitably say the wrong things. People read the story of the man who fell among thieves, and they say that we must live like the good Samaritan. However, in this story, we are portrayed as the man who fell among thieves. We are destined for destruction unless somebody saves us. We're not people who need to save someone else. We are the people who need saving. The good Samaritan portrays Jesus, our savior. That's why the good Samaritan is the one who does the saving.

As the Samaritan was traveling, he saw the man who fell among thieves and had compassion on him. The Samaritan went close to him, poured oil and wine on his wounds, bound him up, set him on his beast, took him to the inn, and cared for him. Then he gave two pence to the innkeeper and told him to take care of him: "Whatever more you spend, I will repay you when I return." The good Samaritan did all these things. But what did the man who fell among thieves do? Nothing at all. Jesus needs to save us.

The Path That Jacob and Esau Walk: Grace and Works

What is the difference between Jacob and Esau? Esau tried to hunt on his own, and then receive the blessing as a wage for the work. However, you can never be saved through that. Salvation is received through grace; it cannot be received as payment for a wage.

Through the story of Jacob and Esau, God is showing us the paths of these two people. Esau is diligent and great, and he worked extremely hard to hunt an animal. Then he cooked it himself and brought it to his father in order to be blessed. But instead of receiving a blessing, he was cursed. It was because he tried to be blessed through works, and not by grace.

In Ephesians chapter 2, verses 8 and 9, it says, *For by grace are ye saved through faith; and that not of yourselves: it is the gift of God: Not of works, lest any man should boast.* We don't do anything at all, Jesus does it all. It's about accepting what Jesus has done as ours and bringing that in front of God. Doing nothing at all makes it grace.

About 25 years ago, I received a watch as a gift while I was in Los Angeles. It was a very nice watch. I've been wearing it for 25 years now. I cannot say how thankful I am. When I travel abroad, I'm afraid I might lose this watch, so I usually leave it at home, and I wear a cheaper watch. Back then, this watch cost about $1,000. And this watch works right now exactly the same as it did back then. But if I paid $1.00 to receive this watch, that means I paid a price for it. If it's going to be grace, not even a small price can be paid for it. It has to be received freely without any wages.

When God saved us from sin, He saved us by grace. If any effort or labor is paid, that is not grace. It cannot be salvation. We have to receive what Jesus has achieved by faith, for free, without doing anything for it. On the contrary, there's nothing received by grace in this world.

If we asked,"Hey, how did you become an honor student?"

We'd hear, "I studied hard."

"How did you make money?"

"I worked hard at my job."

Whatever it is we do, we are paid a wage. Nothing in our lives is done without a wage. However, contrary to the world, there is nothing God gives us as a wage. When you were born, how much did you pay for your handsome face? When you buy a car, the salesman asks you this and that. "What kind of car are you looking for? What kind of options do you want?" Whenever you buy a car, you have to pay a certain price for additional options. Nowadays, cars have so many options. The more you pay, the more comfortable the car. However, how much does a good-looking person pay for the option of a handsome face? How much does a person pay to receive a healthy body? It was all free.

Why was Esau unable to receive the blessing of God? God wants to give us blessings by grace. However, Esau wanted to be blessed through his sweat, labor, and hunting. On the other hand, Jacob did not do any work on his own—he went before Isaac with only what his mother,

Rebekah, did and was blessed as a result. Rebekah cooked, placed Esau's clothes on Jacob, and covered the smooth parts of his neck and arms to make him like Esau. There's nothing that Jacob did at all. He received everything from his mother as grace.

And that is how we are saved. We don't receive salvation by doing something. If our efforts are added, then it is not grace. Therefore, it cannot be salvation. Even if $1 was paid for a $1,000-watch, a price has still been paid. Therefore, it is not grace. A wage must not be paid in any way, shape, or form in order for it to be grace. Grace is receiving everything for free, without paying a price, in any sort of way. However, people don't know this, so they are unable to understand Genesis chapter 27, at all.

It is not easy for Esau to hunt. What do you have to do to catch one deer? First, you would have to track the deer. Then you would have to quietly get close. If it runs away, you have to chase it. And then you have to shoot your arrow accurately. If the arrow hits too low on the fleeing deer, it will still be able to limp away. Then you would have to chase it down and shoot it with another arrow. But even after you hit it again, the deer could still run for a while before collapsing. But the whole, entire time, you have to chase it down. Then, you had to carry that very heavy deer over your shoulders and climb back over the mountains. It's a really hard task. It's very difficult and would cause you to sweat profusely.

That day, Esau went through all of that hard work to catch the deer, make the venison, and bring the meat to his father. However, why was he not blessed? It was because he tried to be blessed as a wage for all the work that he did. God never blesses us as a wage for what we have done. He only gives us grace. That's why Esau was not blessed. However, the only things Jacob brought forth were what his mother prepared for him, and he was blessed. Jacob did not receive blessings as wages for his works—he was blessed by grace.

Many People Who Walk the Path of Esau

Even today, a lot of folks say, "I have to repent with tears. I need to be good from now on, so I can go to heaven," as they continue to commit sins. If people could do something in order to go to heaven, then they would boast, "This is what I did to be saved, you should do this too." God hates this. *Not of works, lest any man should boast. (Ephesians 2:9)* Receiving something through fasting, trying hard, and doing all of that is a wage. What does Romans chapter 4 say about that? *Now to him that worketh is the reward not reckoned of grace, but of debt. (Romans 4:4)* The award or wage received by a person who works is not considered grace, but a debt. Receiving anything through our own works is not grace. They are the wages of our works.

What does verse 5 say? *But to him that worketh not, but believeth on him that justifieth the ungodly, his faith is counted for righteousness. (Romans 4:5)* It says that there is a "he" that justifies the ungodly, and that is God. God says that a person who is ungodly because he has committed sins has been made righteous. If you have committed sins and God says that you are justified by something you did, then that justification is received as a wage, not by grace. Even though we do no works at all, God calls us, who were ungodly, justified. That faith is counted as righteousness to those who have accepted this word.

It's about realizing this: "I don't do something in order to receive salvation, but the blood of Jesus has washed away all my sins. Therefore, I have been made righteous." All we did was commit sins, but God wants to teach us that we have become righteous by grace. That is why He recorded Genesis chapter 27. Esau tried to be blessed as wages for his efforts and works. Ultimately, however, he was not blessed. Jacob did not do anything at all, but because his mother did everything for him, he was blessed through that.

We've done nothing. Instead, Jesus did the work of making us righteous. This is so amazing! When people read Genesis chapter 27 and don't know what it means, they say, "How come Jacob lied, but was blessed? And Esau did good, but was cursed?" However, this story teaches us how we can receive the blessing to go to heaven. Heaven is not received as a wage for what we've done. The person who has done nothing at all receives everything by grace. God gives the people, who have committed sins and has not done any good, the grace of salvation. On the other hand, God does not give this to the people who have done good. You should not be saying, "God, I prayed. I fasted. I gave offerings," in order to be saved. Throw all of that away. Salvation must be received by grace. Jesus died on the cross instead of us. Jesus paid the entire price for sins we needed to pay. That's why if you try to pay the price for your sins, you can't receive salvation by grace.

If you do good, then you can never receive grace. You should do nothing at all. The Bible says, "Now to him that worketh is the reward not reckoned of grace, but of debt." God only wants to save us by grace. If you pay something, God does not save you. Today, it is not that people do not get saved by doing wrong—the fact is they do too well.

We truly receive salvation by grace, without doing anything. It's so amazing. Have you done good? Have you kept the law? Have you given an offering? Have you helped your neighbors? Erase all of that from your heart. If you do those things, you have the heart, "Oh, God will bless me because I did this and that." God hates that heart the most.

God wants to give everything to us by grace. Esau was cursed, and Jacob was blessed. Just as Jacob's mother did all the work for Jacob, Jesus has done all the work so that we could receive the blessings. Have you committed sins? Jesus has washed them clean. As we live in this world, we have to do the work ourselves to receive a wage. People, who are used to such ways of Satan, they think that even the blessing of God is something you're supposed to receive by doing something. If people follow those thoughts, they will never receive salvation. Salvation is by grace. Without works, without effort, and without labor, salvation is given 100% free by grace. When people try to do good themselves, it breaks up the grace. They're unable to receive grace. Satan deceives us to keep us from being saved. He deceives us, saying, "You have to try hard to receive salvation." However, if you try hard, then you're paying a wage. God cannot save you like that. This is the truth that I discovered as I continued to read the Bible.

Be People Who Know the Truth, and Receive Grace According to the Word

Even though we have not done any good, even though we have not made any effort, and all we did was evil, Jesus died on the cross, and delivered us from sin. Even though man appears to be good, man is only slightly good. No one is completely good. That is why we should not exert our own goodness. We are all dirty, filthy sinners. Jesus washed our sins as white as snow, and He made us holy. Is there anyone among you who thinks that you got saved through your hard work? Did your sins get washed away through an all-night prayer? If you think that, it's a lie. That is different from the words of God.

For by grace are ye saved through faith; and that not of yourselves: it is the gift of God: Not of works, lest any many should boast. (Ephesians 2:8-9)

Now to him that worketh is the reward not reckoned of grace, but of debt. But to him that worketh not, but believeth on him that justifieth the ungodly, his faith is counted for righteousness. (Romans 4:4-5)

Though we did not do any good, and all we did was sin, God says that we are righteous. Believing means having the heart, "If God says that I'm righteous, then I am righteous." Jacob was the one who was blessed. Jacob did not do anything at all. He took what his mother prepared, went before his father, and presented everything to him. Nobody among us can be saved without grace. We are saved through believing in what Jesus achieved.

When you come to know the truth the Bible speaks about, you will receive the forgiveness of sins by grace, apart from works. Jesus washed the sins of a dirty person like me, and God has made me righteous for free. I give thanks to God, who has allowed me to believe in this truth so that I could receive salvation. I hope that you will not look at yourself, but take the work that Jesus has done before God and receive that grace.